MW01025705

*For
Kirk &
Covenant*

For Kirk & Covenant

THE STALWART COURAGE OF JOHN KNOX

DOUGLAS WILSON

LEADERS IN ACTION
GENERAL EDITOR, GEORGE GRANT

HIGHLAND BOOKS

CUMBERLAND HOUSE • NASHVILLE, TENNESSEE

Published by Cumberland House Publishing, Inc., 431 Harding Industrial Drive, Nashville, Tennessee 37211.

Cover photo from an engraving by J. C. Armytage based upon the portrait in Verheiden, ca. 1602.

Unless otherwise noted, Scripture references are from the New King James Version (NKJV) Copyright © 1979, 1980, 1982 by Thomas Nelson, Inc., Publishers. Used by permission.

Library of Congress Cataloging-in-Publication Data

Wilson, Douglas, 1953–
    For kirk and covenant : the stalwart courage of
        John Knox / Douglas Wilson.
            p.   cm. — (Leaders in action series)
    Includes bibliographical references.
    ISBN 1-58182-058-5 (alk. paper)
    1. Knox, John, ca. 1514–1572. 2. Reformation—Scot-
land—Biography. I. Title. II. Series.
BX9223.W55 2000
285'.2'092—dc21
    [B]   00-027356

Printed in the United States of America

2 3 4 5 6 7 8 9—04 03 02 01

For my first grandson,
Knox Alexander Merkle
May you soon take your place in the long battle,
and fight as honestly as your namesake.

Contents

FOREWORD

*T*HE GREAT nineteenth century historian, Thomas Carlyle, though himself alienated from his native church was an enthusiastic admirer of its founder, John Knox. He was, he asserted, "a most surprising individual to have kindled all Scotland, within a few years, almost within a few months, into perhaps the noblest flame of sacred human zeal and brave determination to believe only what it found completely believable, and to defy the whole world and the devil at its back, in unsubduable defense of the same."

Knox was, to Carlyle, the very epitome of stalwart leadership, "Here is a gentleman seemingly of eupeptic, not to say stolid and thoughtless frame of mind; much at ease in Zion, and content to take things as they come, if only they will let him digest his victuals, and sleep in a whole skin. Knox, you can well perceive, in all his writings and in all his way of life, was emphatically of Scottish build; eminently a national specimen; in fact what we might denominate the most Scottish of Scots, and to this day typical of all the qualities which belong nationally to the very choicest of Scotsmen we have known, or had a clear record of; utmost sharpness of discernment and discrimination, courage enough, and, what is still better, no particular consciousness of courage, but a readiness in all simplicity to do and dare whatsoever is commanded by the inward voice of native manhood; on the whole a beautiful and simple but complete incompatibility with whatever is false in word or conduct; inexorable contempt and detestation of what in modern speech is called humbug. Nothing hypocritical, foolish or untrue can find harbor in this man; a pure, and mainly silent, tenderness of affection is in him, touches of genial humor are not wanting under his severe austerity; an occasional growl of sarcastic indignation against malfeasance, falsity, and stupidity; indeed, secretly an extensive fund of that disposition, kept mainly silent, though inwardly in daily exercise; a most clear-cut, hardy, distinct, and effective man; fearing God and without any other fear."

Carlyle was invariably impressed by such stalwart leadership traits. And to be sure there is a power in unswerving conviction that inevitably arrests the attentions of both men and nations. There is an almost indescribable appeal that attaches itself to uncompromising vision and principled passion. This fact was undoubtedly illustrated quite vividly all throughout the life and work of John Knox.

His unswerving commitment and his righteous determination were indeed, inimitable. Like Daniel in the Old Testament, he was forthright in his condemnation of sin (Daniel 4:27), unguarded in his pronouncement of truth (Daniel 5:13–28), and single-minded in his adherence to the Word of God (Daniel 6:5). Like King Josiah in ancient Israel, he did what was right in the sight of the Lord, never turning aside to the right hand or to the left (2 Kings 22:2). Like the great general Joshua, he dutifully obeyed the clear commands of Scripture, always steadfast and unwavering (Joshua 23:6,8).

But, such character traits and such stands, however compelling, are inevitably costly. It nearly cost Knox everything during his lifetime and it has earned him the odium and ire of virtually every secular historian in the years since—Carlyle stands nearly alone in praising him. A simple compromise here or there might well have saved him from imprisonment, exile, and anathema. But he refused to compromise. He could have tried to work within the system. He could have tried conciliation, accommodation, or negotiation. But he refused to compromise, risking everything for the sake of principle.

The uncompromising stance of leaders like Knox is more often than not mistaken for prideful self-assurance. Unlike Carlyle, most observers take Knox's refusal to compromise to be little more than hardheaded stubbornness. They presume that he was just another in a long line of self-confident, egotistical, and pertinacious dogmatists—a dangerous, humorless, and acrimonious Ayatollah-like figure.

In the Bible, Joseph's enemies thought the same thing (Genesis 37:8). They assumed that he was a swaggering, self-promoting braggart—an irascible, irrational, and intractable man blinded by presumption and self-importance. Indeed, virtually all of the heroic leaders of redemptive history have been accused of having a self-indulgent, self-inflating, and self-assuming attitude: Moses (Ezekiel 2:14), Job (Job 8:2), David (1 Samuel 18:8), and even Jesus (Matthew 9:3). Uncompromising steadfastness is almost always confused with unreasoning pontification. Righteousness is thus often labeled as a kind of unyielding intolerance, and righteous men and women are popularly diagnosed as suffering from delusions of grandeur.

But nothing could be further from the truth.

Those uncompromising leaders throughout the ages who have conquered kingdoms, performed acts of righteousness, obtained promises, shut the mouths of lions, quenched the power of fire, escaped the edge of the sword, and from weakness were made strong, did so by faith (Hebrews 11:33–34). In other words, they trusted God rather than themselves. Far from having confidence or certainty in their own flesh, their own ideas, their own understanding, their own abilities, their own strength, and their own ingenuity, they put their full reliance on God (Philippians 3:3). They obtained victory even amidst travail, not because they were domineeringly proud, but because they were submissively humble (Matthew 5:3–12).

Thus the reason Knox—like each of the great leaders in whose footsteps he was following—was able to square off against the forces of evil without compromise involved not only what he knew, but what he was. Living by faith, walking in steadfastness, and partaking of resurrection power is completely and entirely dependent on righteous humility. Knox certainly comprehended the fact that a leader must "speak boldly" (Titus 3:8), "confidently" (Ephesians 6:20), and "without fear" (Philippians 1:14). But he also knew that he had to speak the truth in love (Ephesians 4:15).

Though books on the life and work of Knox abound, rarely has this perspective been adequately portrayed—even by such admirers as Carlyle. But Douglas Wilson has not only captured the real essence of Knox's life, his times, his leadership traits, and his continuing legacy, he has apprehended that essential tenacity rooted in humility that so marked his ministry and message.

For Kirk and Covenant is the eighth volume in a series of books profiling the characteristics of the greatest leaders in the history of Christendom. Though containing certain biographical elements, the books are not intended to be traditional biographies. Instead, in this over-managed, under-led day, they are designed to point us toward greater substance and surer maturity. I can think of no one better qualified to tackle such a issue, in such a fashion, utilizing such a subject, in such a time than Douglas Wilson—in many ways, a contemporary Knox. As you read the uncompromising, yet humble message inscribed on these pages, I think you'll quickly see why. And I think you'll readily, heartily, and gratefully agree.

—George Grant

ACKNOWLEDGMENTS

$\mathcal{M}$Y DEBTS are too great to discharge in such a small space, but I must attempt it just the same. Appearances must be kept up. But despite this duty, the great danger in such acknowledgments is really the possibility it creates for gross sins of omission. My intellectual debts really are too great to take care of in any adequate fashion here. Nonetheless, here goes.

It is my privilege to minister to the wonderful congregation of Christian saints at Christ Church. They pray and labor as genuine Christians should in the ministry and work of the kingdom of God. The elders and deacons of our church have supplied great support and encouragement in the work I have been called to do.

I am grateful to Douglas Jones, who works down the hall, and has served as an intellectual sounding board on many issues. He has been particularly helpful with the historical context surrounding the material in this book.

Many thanks go to George Grant, who was kind enough to invite me to participate in this project. I have enjoyed working with him very much and look forward to our continued work together in various settings.

My parents taught me to love books and the many people I would meet in them. In so doing, they have introduced me to countless good teachers and examples.

My dear wife was kind enough to tell me when the first draft of a chapter wasn't any good. She has a quick mind, merciless red pen, and a tender, helpful spirit. Having seen how fortunate John Knox was in marriage has made me doubly grateful for how blessed I have been in mine.

INTRODUCTION

*D*OROTHY PARKER, the great American wit, once wrote a poem called "Partial Comfort" that gave voice to a very common assumption about John Knox.

Whose love is given over-well
Shall look on Helen's face in hell,
Whilst they whose love is thin and wise
May view John Knox in paradise.[1]

The snide slander easily sells; for a number of centuries now John Knox has been a harsh and frightening figure used to keep small children from wandering off into the woods. Jesus taught us that we should beware when all men speak well of us; the chastisement implied in our Lord's comment does not appear to apply to John Knox in any way. In this world anyway, Knox is not a figure who would attract universal acclaim.

Even an observer like C.S. Lewis, normally insightful on such matters, comments on Knox as a man who did not understand himself. When Knox lamented his inclination to temporize, Lewis comments, "One is tempted to say that no equal instance of self-ignorance is recorded until the moment at which [Samuel] Johnson pronounced himself 'a very polite man.'"[2] But of course, the two situations are not comparable at all. Johnson, openly rude, thought himself openly polite. Knox, openly courageous and bold, knew his own heart's temptation to shrink from the fight— and he is the only one who *could* know them. The gulf is a wide one that separates self-ignorance from victory over whispering temptations.

Among the historically literate, both his accusers and defenders frequently share these widespread assumptions about Knox. His attackers write him off as a religious fanatic; his modern defenders are perhaps too prone to defend him as a hard man necessary for hard times. But such a pragmatic defense is hardly Christian. If something is wrong, it is wrong all the time. If it is right, it deserves to be defended, regardless of how unpopular the defense might be.

However, I spoke of historical literacy, which, I fear, is far less common than it used to be. In one sense, this modern disparagement of history has provided us with an unexpected blessing. Although originally employed as a means of robbing us of our heritage, we may be grateful that some persistent slanders have been erased as well. This enables us to turn to our subject—the life and example of a very great man indeed—the tender and courageous Christian named John Knox.

CHRONOLOGY

1549	Released from galley slavery, Knox begins pastoring in Berwick, England; Thomas Cranmer publishes the first *Book of Common Prayer*
1550	Meets his future wife, Marjory Bowes; Knox appears at Newcastle to defend his teaching that the Mass is idolatry
1551	Knox is appointed to be one of King Edward's chaplains by the privy council
1552	Moves to London and refuses the bishopric of Rochester
1553	Forced into exile when Mary Tudor assumes the throne
1554	Visits Calvin's Geneva, and becomes a pastor for some Marian exiles in Frankfurt
1555	Dispute in the Frankfurt church forces him to Geneva; pastors an English congregation there, marries Marjory Bowes, and returns secretly to Scotland
1556	Returns to Geneva and is condemned for heresy in Scotland
1557	Knox attempts, unsuccessfully, to return to Scotland
1558	Writes the *First Blast of the Trumpet* against the tyranny of Mary Tudor; Elizabeth I becomes queen of England
1559	Returns to Scotland, and begins the work of reformation in earnest; Knox preaches at St. Andrews
1560	The Parliament in Scotland adopts the Protestant "Scots Confession;" Marjory Knox dies, leaving John Knox with two sons; Knox's *Treatise on Predestination* is published in Geneva; the Geneva Bible is also published, the work of the English congregation that Knox had pastored
1561	Knox helps to write the *First Book of Discipline*; Mary Queen of Scots, assumes the throne in Scotland; Knox has his first interview with Mary
1562	Knox debates with Quintin Kennedy, the abbot of Crossraguell
1562–4	The Roman Catholic Council of Trent
1563	Foxe writes his famous *Book of Martyrs*
1564	Knox marries Margaret Ochiltree (Stuart); she comes to bear him three daughters

1565   Knox preaches a controversial sermon in the hearing of Lord Darnley, the new husband of Mary; Knox is consequently summoned before the privy council

1566   Knox writes most of his *History of the Reformation in Scotland*

1567   Lord Darnley is murdered; Mary and Bothwell marry shortly thereafter; Bothwell flees to Denmark, Mary is imprisoned, and abdicates the throne to her young son, James; Knox preaches the coronation sermon; James Stuart, Mary's half-brother, becomes regent of Scotland

1568   Mary escapes and flees to England, where she is imprisoned for almost twenty years, and then executed; James Stuart is assassinated

1570   Knox suffers a stroke, but is still able to preach occasionally

1571   Because of political turmoil, Knox moves to St. Andrews

1572   When order is restored, Knox returns to and dies in Edinburgh, and is buried at St. Giles

*For
Kirk &
Covenant*

PART 1
THE LIFE OF JOHN KNOX

O God, give me Scotland or I die!

—John Knox

For if the fire be without heat, or the burning lamp without light,
then true faith may be without fervent prayer.

—John Knox

And here I call my God to record that neither profit to myself,
hatred of any person or persons, nor affection or favour
that I bear towards any private man,
causes me this day to speak as you have heard.

—John Knox

Understanding the Times

*B*Y ANY reckoning, Scotland was a spiritual badlands. The people were barbaric and superstitious, the clergy were grossly immoral, and rank ignorance of biblical truth had settled in holy places ostensibly dedicated to the preservation of God's Word. The Church was the center of Scottish medieval life, and that Church was thoroughly corrupt. Of this time, Thomas McCrie observed, "The kingdom swarmed with ignorant, idle, luxurious monks, who, like locusts, devoured the fruits of the earth, and filled the air with pestilential infection."[1]

The fact of this ecclesiastical corruption is not a "view" held only by those sympathetic to the doctrines of the Reformation; the widespread corruption was simply a fact, acknowledged by honest men on both sides. A very able and winsome Roman priest named Ninan Winzet, a strong opponent of Knox, admitted that this gross and blackened condition of the Church provoked the Reformation. He acknowledged that the bishops and clergy in the age prior to the Reformation were "ignorant or vicious, or both," and were "unworthy the name of pastors."[2]

In this climate of darkness, a young nobleman of royal lineage named Patrick Hamilton became the first prominent martyr of the Reformation in Scotland. Born in 1504, he was set apart to the clergy according to the custom of the times— the abbacy of Ferne bestowed upon him in his childhood. Such "livings" were not opportunities for feeding the flock of Christ; rather, they were a source of a predictable and easy income. Nevertheless, as early as 1526, light began to dawn in his mind. His condemnations of the clerical corruption aroused some suspicion, and so he left Scotland to travel on the Continent. An act of Parliament on July 17, 1525, had banned the importation of Luther's books into Scotland, a land that had always, as they put it, "bene clene of all sic filth and vice." The connection between the circulation of such material and the dawning light in Patrick Hamilton's mind is not hard to imagine.

While on the Continent, he found his way to Wittenberg, where he met with both Luther and Melancthon, impressing them both with his zeal. After studying a short time at the university in Marburg, he, being a zealous young man, determined to return to Scotland with the gospel. Upon his arrival, Archbishop Beaton betrayed him and threw him into prison.[3] At his trial, he defended himself with remarkable courage and patience. He was condemned and consigned to the flames on the last day of February in 1528. At this time, John Knox was about thirteen years old. The martyr was not very old himself, only twenty-four when he died. His last words were, "How long, O Lord, shall darkness cover this realm! How long wilt thou suffer this tyranny of men! Lord Jesus, receive my spirit!"[4]

A martyr of noble birth created even more interest in the new doctrines. The "novel" opinions continued to spread, and the officials, alarmed, adopted a policy of vigorous persecution. In the decade between 1530 and 1540, many able and honest men gave their lives for confessing the truth. Numerous others fled to the Continent, few of them ever returning. During this time, it does not appear that there was a single public teacher of the truth in Scotland. The Word spread rapidly anyway, largely due to the importation of Tyndale's translation of the Scriptures, along with many Protestant books.

The authorities resisted this new knowledge with a stiff, bloodthirsty, and unyielding blindness. Bishop Crighton of Dunkeld is reported by Foxe as saying that he thanked God that he "never knew what the Old and New Testaments were." Even if the incident is accounted apocryphal, the fact that the expression subsequently became proverbial in Scotland indicated how widespread such clerical ignorance was. Though deplorably ignorant of the Bible, the ecclesiastical officials nonetheless clearly understood the threat presented by the new Protestant doctrines. In response to that threat, the authorities were quite prepared to use as much force as they thought it might take.

As events turned out, it took more than they had. The pressures building toward reformation were enormous. Another important force preparing for the Reformation was, surprisingly, the work of poets and playwrights. A corrupt clergy is always good for a few laughs. Those with the power to persecute were forced to tolerate ridicule of this form in a way they did not tolerate midnight Bible readings. Her own corruption and the widespread mockery of that corruption greatly diminished the moral authority of the Church. The bishops repeatedly sought laws against such lampooning, but the mockery was impossible to stop. Just imagine today a law forbidding any jokes at the expense of televangelists.

By 1540, a reforming zeal was widespread among a multitude of commoners and a significant number of the Scottish nobility. As the later history of the reformation in Scotland shows, some of the nobility were motivated by a hunger for church lands, and it has been easy for some to dismiss the Reformation because of this obvious greed factor. It is true that the Reformation was manipulated, later, by some, but at this early date an acceptance of the gospel was much more likely to end in fire or exile than in rich, landed estates. The Reformation in Scotland was born and nourished through a hunger for truth.

Before turning to consider the life and leadership of John Knox during this time, one must address another background consideration. Many have difficulty understanding this era because they have never successfully identified all the key figures—particularly all the Marys. As the fellow once said, you can't tell the players without a scorecard.

Mary of Guise was the queen-regent who ruled Scotland after the death of her husband, James V of Scotland. Their daughter, named Mary as well, was taken to France and raised there in the Roman Catholic faith. When she returned in 1561 and ascended the throne of Scotland she became known as Mary Queen of Scots. Neither mother nor daughter should be confused with Queen Mary of England who reigned from to 1553 to 1558, and because of her persecuting zeal against the Protestants, became known as Bloody Mary. After her death, she was succeeded by Elizabeth I.[5] John Knox was exiled from Scotland under Mary of Guise, fled from England when Bloody Mary took the throne, and returned to Scotland for his famous encounters with Mary Queen of Scots.

Mary Queen of Scots married the nobleman Lord Darnley, and their child became (in his infancy) James VI of Scotland, crowned in infancy. John Knox preached his coronation sermon. Later, after the death of Elizabeth of England, James assumed the crown of England as well, becoming James I of England—the well-known James of the King James Version of the Bible.

Various spellings and titles cause another minor problem for moderns. For example, Mary Queen of Scots had a half brother named James Stuart. In some sources his name is spelled James Stewart, and because he became the earl of Moray, he is also called Moray (or Murray). During the minority of James VI, he was appointed to rule Scotland as regent. It is not hard to see how the modern reader might find himself reading about the same individual under many differing descriptions.

The story before us is a fascinating and exciting one. With these and other minor distractions set aside, we should find the biblical lessons in the courageous leadership of John Knox to be inspiring indeed.

EARLY LIFE AND EDUCATION

*D*ETAILS ABOUT Knox's early life are few, and some are contradictory. Early biographers believed John Knox was born around 1505, but the consensus now is that he was born c. 1515,[6] probably at Haddington.

Though he obviously received a liberal education, where he was educated is also uncertain. Theodore Beza, a contemporary of Knox, says that he studied under John Major at the University of St. Andrews, but there is no record of him having matriculated in the defective records of St. Andrews. A certain John Knox entered the University of Glasgow in 1522, but for various reasons, this is not likely to be our Knox. All in all, Knox probably studied at St. Andrews.

He studied under John Major, who was one of the great scholastic minds of the time. Major was a very capable exponent of a particular view of church government which denied supremacy to the papacy, and John Knox, and his peer George Buchanan, who also studied under Major, learned some of these early lessons very well.[7] But John

Knox soon began to reject the convoluted scholasticism which dominated academic circles at that time, and turned his attention *ad fontes,* back to the original sources of Scripture and the early fathers. Although better than many of his time, in this respect, Major was also capable of scholastic gnat-strangling, and Knox soon turned away from this aspect of his instructor's teaching.

Far from being a rejection of church tradition, the Reformation was a self-conscious return to earlier traditions—the teachings of the New Testament and the early church fathers. One historical observer makes this very important point:

> *New reforms were initiated in the leading cities of the Reformation which reflected the conviction that pure worship must be "according to the Scripture," and consequently simple, spiritual, and intelligent. Intensive study of Scripture* and Patristic sources *over the next two decades, as well as regular interaction among the leading reformers resulted in a more thorough reform.*[8]

This impulse to return to the ways of the ancient church was strong in Knox. He was not content with the excerpts of the fathers contained in medieval anthologies, so he sought out the original works, in particular the works of Jerome and Augustine. As McCrie points out, in Jerome he found a method of study which greatly attracted him—returning to the Scriptures as the source of all truth, and an emphasis on studying them in the original languages. From reading Augustine, Knox quickly learned how a man may be greatly honored in name while studiously ignored in substance. These profound intellectual influences were beginning to accumulate in Knox before he broke with the Roman Catholic church. He was a reformation waiting to happen.

He began working as a papal cleric around 1540. Just a few years later, in 1543, he gave up this position. Some time prior to 1540, Knox had been ordained as a Roman Catholic priest. As late as 1543, he had still signed himself as a "Minister of the Holy Altar." He gave no *public* support to the cause of the Reformation until 1545. These years were obviously the years of transition, with Knox's conversion probably occurring sometime around 1543. Somewhere in this time period, John Knox first heard the gospel from a preacher named Thomas Guillaume (or Williams). This preacher had been a prominent Black Friar, of the Dominican order, but had come to embrace the sentiments of the reformers. As a result of Knox's conversion, Cardinal Beaton condemned him as a heretic and employed assassins to waylay him. The Lord brought him under the protection of Hugh Douglas of Langniddrie, and his life was spared.

In understanding Knox's conversion we have to understand far more than what modern evangelicals would call a "personal testimony." There were, of course, the personal elements present, but there were profound cultural aspects to it as well. The new learning of the Renaissance and the Reformation (which were not so tidily separated at that time as they are now in Survey of European History courses) had an intoxicating effect. In addition, the sense of sheer cultural liberation from a millennium of efforts at self-salvation was monumental. As C.S. Lewis stated it, "We want, above all, to know what it felt like to be an early Protestant." We moderns would have said here, influenced by our strong individualism, "what it felt like to be a new Christian," but far more is involved than just personal liberation. Continuing, Lewis says this:

> *All the initiative has been on God's side; all has been free, unbounded grace. And all will continue to be free, unbounded grace. His own puny and ridiculous efforts would be as helpless to retain the joy as they would have been to achieve it in the first place . . . He is not saved because he does works of love: he does works of love because he is saved. It is faith alone that has saved him: faith bestowed by sheer gift. From this buoyant humility, this farewell to the self with all its good resolutions, anxiety, scruples, and motive-scratchings, all the Protestant doctrines originally sprang.* [9]

Buoyant humility. This understanding of grace was immediately and radically applied to the world by the early Reformers. They looked beyond their own individual circumstances. In this respect, medieval men saw that their newly-recovered faith had to be understood as a public possession, and this is why there was an enormous cultural convulsion.

In 1542, James V of Scotland died after a disastrous raid on the English, which threw Scotland into political turmoil. During the last two years of his reign, the number of Protestants had been increasing significantly, and the established clergy were urging James V to undertake quite a vigorous persecution. The death of James left the two factions at a standoff.

The earl of Arran, a very vocal Protestant, became regent of Scotland. However, in the Scotland of that day treachery was an art form, and the earl soon publicly abjured the reformed religion. Negotiations to marry the future Queen of Scots (still in her childhood) to Edward, the son of Henry VIII of Protestant England, were consequently broken off. Soon after this, the young Mary was betrothed to the Dauphin of France, and was sent there to be reared and educated. Her upbringing there in a court thoroughly loyal to the papacy was to have a profound impact on Scotland in the years to come.

At this critical time for Scotland, we find the first appearance of John Knox standing with the cause of the Reformation, but surprisingly, not in the pulpit.

WISHART'S BODYGUARD

*G*EORGE WISHART had been teaching the Greek Testament in Montrose, and suspicion of heresy soon fell on him. The bishop of Brechin summoned Wishart, but he withdrew instead to England. He resided for about six years at the University at Cambridge. He returned to Scotland in 1544 and began an itinerant preaching ministry. He returned to a tempestuous situation, but was not of a tumultuous spirit himself.

We have two accounts of Wishart's character, one from John Knox, and the other from a student of Wishart's at Cambridge named Emery Tylney. According to Tylney, Wishart was "courteous, lowly, lovely, glad to teach, desirous to learn." Knox paints a similar portrait: "a man of such graces as befoir him war never hard within this realm, yea, and ar rare to be found yit in any man, nochtwithstanding this great lyght of God that sence his dayis hes schyned unto us."[10]

Scotland was in turmoil for a number of reasons, political and religious together. After the death of James V, the nation divided into two factions. One party aligned with France, and the other party favored England. The established Church was a strong advocate of the French alliance, with the Protestants sympathetic to Protestant England. At the same time, the position of the Protestants was tenuous because England was in truth Scotland's historical adversary, and the ambitions of England's king, Henry VIII, made the situation even more complicated. It would probably not have taken a lot to convince Henry to ascend the throne of Scotland, had it been offered. The pride of England made even some of the Protestants nervous. There is good reason to believe that Knox was in this number.

There were wheels with wheels. The earl of Arran recanted his Protestantism in part because he was alarmed at an argument presented to him by his illegitimate brother, John Hamilton. "He alarmed Arran by reminding him that the legality of his mother's marriage, and therefore his own legitimacy, depended on the validity of the divorce granted by the Pope to his father from a former wife. If the papal authority . . . were repudiated by Scotland, then the Regent was a bastard with no legal claim either to the earldom, to the regency, or . . . to the throne."[11] All this serves to show how tangled the religious, personal, and political questions were—possible to distinguish, but impossible to separate.

So when George Wishart returned to Scotland, the party favoring France was in power, but certain powerful lords of the English faction afforded him some measure of protection. One of those lords was Hugh Douglas, protector of John Knox, and father of the boys whom Knox was tutoring. During a five-week stay in Lothian, Wishart stayed at the house of Douglas. Knox had many opportunities to hear him preach, and to confer with him privately.

Whenever Wishart was preaching in his area of the country, Knox accompanied and heard him gladly. During a visit to Dundee, Knox described a very serious situation with the dry humor of Scots understatement.

> *While he was spending his life to comfort the afflicted,*
> *the Devil ceased not to stir up his own son the*
> *Cardinal again, who corrupted by money a desperate*
> *priest named sir John Wigton, to slay the said master*
> *George, who looked not to himself in all things so*
> *circumspectly as worldly men would have wished.* [12]

Knox went on to recount how this priest approached Wishart with a short sword under his gown. Wishart saw him and said, "My friend, what would ye do?" and put his hand on the priest's hand and took his dagger from him. The priest confessed what he was about to do, and the surrounding crowd grew violent, and demanded the traitor be delivered over to them. But Wishart took the aspiring assassin in his arms and said, "Whosoever troubles him shall trouble me; for he has hurt me in nothing, but he has done great comfort both to you and me, to wit, he has let us understand what we may fear in times to come. We will watch better." And so he saved the life of the one who was going to take his.

The resolution to "watch better" was also remembered. After the assassination attempt at Dundee, a bodyguard was assigned to protect Wishart. In the accounts, we see that role falling to Knox, who carried a two-handed broadsword to protect the evangelist. On the night Wishart was captured, he directed that this sword be taken away from Knox. The latter asked permission to accompany him to his next destination, which Wishart denied. By this time, Wishart was under a very strong burden, a heavy presentiment of his approaching martyrdom. He told Knox, "Nay, return to your bairnes, and God bless you: ane is sufficient for a sacrifice."[13]

The earl of Bothwell betrayed Wishart, and he was delivered into the hands of the cardinal. Then given a mock trial, in which he was insulted and spat upon by his judges, Wishart was condemned to the stake as an obstinate heretic. He was scheduled to be executed near the Castle of St. Andrews, with all the guns of the castle trained on the place to prevent any attempted rescue from any quarter. The front tower of the palace was decked out with cushions and tapestries so that the cardinal and his clergy could enjoy the show.

Wishart gave his last testimony as the fire was lit. "This flame hath scorched my body, yet hath it not daunted my spirit. But he who from yonder high place beholdest us with such pride, shall, within a few days, lie in the same as ignominiously as now he is seen proudly to rest himself."[14] The fire started, Wishart was mercifully strangled, and the fire consumed his body, but this remarkable prophecy at the close of his life came to an astonishing fulfillment, and was closely connected to John Knox's call to the ministry.

THE ASSASSINATION

*J*UST SEVERAL months after Wishart's execution, the Castle at St. Andrews was captured by a band of Protestant conspirators. One of the chief conspirators was a man named John Leslie, who had vowed to avenge the death of Wishart. A report of trouble had come to the cardinal's ears, but he thought himself completely secure in his castle.

The conspirators approached the castle early on a Saturday morning. The prior evening, the cardinal "had been busy at his accounts with Mistress Marion Ogilvy that night," as Knox put it.[15] About sixteen men surprised the porter and forced their way into the castle. The cardinal, awakened by the shouting, asked from the window what the noise meant. The reply came that the castle had been taken, and so the cardinal locked himself in his chamber, piled furniture against the door, and armed himself with a two-handed sword.

John Leslie came to the door, and demanded to be let in. The cardinal refused and fire was brought, and either the cardinal or his chamber child opened the door. The cardinal cried out, "I am a priest; I am a priest: ye will not slay me." John Leslie struck him, as did another conspirator, but a third man, James Melville, perceiving them to be "in a choler," pulled them back. He said, "This work and judgment of God (although it be secret) ought to be done with greater gravity."

Melville then presented the cardinal with the point of the sword, and asked, "Repent thee of thy former wicked life, but especially of the shedding of the blood of that notable instrument of God, Master George Wishart, which albeit the flame of fire consumed before men, yet cries it a vengeance upon thee, and we from God are sent to revenge it: For here, before my God, I protest, that neither the [hatred] of thy person, the love of thy riches, nor the fear of any trouble thou could have done to me in particular, moved, nor moves me to strike thee; but only because thou hast been, and remain an obstinate enemy against Christ Jesus and his holy Evangel." Then, as Knox relates the story, Melville struck the cardinal two or three times. The cardinal cried out, "I am a priest, I am a priest: fye, fye: all is gone."[16]

A commotion arose in the town and people gathered outside the wall. They were told to disperse because the cardinal was dead, but the people said they would not go unless they saw him. So, the body of the cardinal was brought to the wall, and he was shown dead over the wall—and the words of the martyr Wishart came to a very unusual fulfillment.

While Knox was not involved in this conspiracy against the cardinal's life, there is no question but that he heartily approved of it. After his description of the death of the cardinal, he stops to give an important warning:

> *These things we write merrily. But we would that the Reader should observe God's just judgments, and how*

*that he can deprehend the worldly wise in their own
wisdom, make their table to be a snare to trap their
own feet, and their own presupposed strength to be
their own destruction. These are the works of our God,
whereby he would admonish the tyrants of this earth,
that in the end he will be revenged of their cruelty,
what strength so ever they make in the contrary.* [17]

This approach is honestly problematic for many modern
Christians. Commenting on Knox's "boisterous and ferocious"
sense of humor, C.S. Lewis says this of Knox's comment that
he was writing "merrily"—"He was apparently afraid lest the
fun of the thing might lead us to forget that even an assassination may have its serious side."[18] The whole incident seems
surreal to us.

On this question, Knox was certainly able to defend
himself ably with an appeal to biblical precedent—the example of Ehud comes to mind—but the problem still nags at
us. Too often, at this point, even men who appreciate Knox
will back away. They will say, for example, that Knox was
essentially a man of his time.[19] This is quite true, but also
beside the point. Was it right or wrong according to the only
final standard that Knox would accept, which is to say the
Word of God? However, even here the problem seems to us
to be even worse. How can we even think about justifying
the shedding of blood in the name of the Bible?

Beneath our difficulty with this situation, we should not
be surprised to find a tangled raft of contemporary assumptions. For a good example of this, contrast our problem with
our response to the life of Dietrich Bonhoffer. A valiant
German pastor, he distinguished himself in his opposition to
Hitler, and early in the war became a conspirator against the
Third Reich. He worked as a courier for a group which made

an attempt on Hitler's life in 1944. His connection with the plot was discovered, and he was executed in 1945.[20]

Although Bonhoffer faced stiff opposition in his own time, in his own nation, in the aftermath of the war, Christians have almost universally applauded him for his role in the assassination attempt. Faith without works is dead.

This does not trouble us because we all know how evil Hitler was. Therefore, this necessarily means that our problem is not with assassination *per se.* Rather our problem has more to do with the standard used to make the determination. Somewhere C.S. Lewis makes a comment relevant to this discussion when he says that we moderns like to take credit for not burning witches, but the reason we do not burn them, he argues, is that we do not believe in them. We *do* execute traitors, Lewis observed, because we all recognize the damage a traitor can do.

We all understand how evil Hitler was, and so we admire Bonhoffer, but well-trained by the assumptions of modernity, we do not understand the context of the Reformation, and the nature of the conflict whenever it came to blood. "Usually brutal arrogance in the judge confronts brutal courage in the prisoner."[21] We believe all religious disputes are in the last analysis debates over nothing, and because we have forgotten the history of our culture, we are unaware of how massive the machinery of oppression was in Knox's day. Thus Knox's approval of this event is seen as that of a religious fanatic and not as that of a freedom fighter.

The wickedness of this particular cardinal was notorious. He was not simply corrupt, but bloodthirsty as well. To take just one example of his character, once while traveling, he instigated the governor to hang four honest men for eating a goose on Friday. He even had a young woman drowned, because she refused to pray to "our Lady" during the birth of her child.

Knox reported that the woman, "having a souchking babe upon hir briest, was drounit."[22]

One final thought is perhaps worth considering. Because Knox was a man of his times, he did share certain blind spots and assumptions with his contemporaries, but he also had a much better view of the evil he was fighting than we do. 500 years from now, we should not be surprised if some Christians have a problem with Bonhoffer as well—trying to kill someone over a mere "political" difference.

CALL TO THE MINISTRY

*A*FTER THE death of the cardinal, the conspirators—
the Castilians—remained holed up in the castle.
The castle was formidable and easy to defend. In addition,
the assassins had taken James, Lord Hamilton, at that time a
boy about eight years old, as a hostage.[23] As with some
modern hostage situations, a negotiated agreement was
worked out, which included as one of its terms the settlement that the Castilians would keep the castle until
the "Governor and the authority of Scotland" could obtain
an absolution for them from the Pope for the killing of
the cardinal.[24]

In the meantime, John Knox was moving around Scotland.
Because he was a wanted man, he "wearied of removing from
place to place," and eventually decided to take refuge in the
castle. The fathers of the boys he had been tutoring before
encouraged him to take refuge there so that he would have the
protection of the castle, and the boys would have the benefit of
hearing him teach again.

So Knox resumed his instruction of the boys at the castle, which he says included work for the boys in their "grammar, and other humane authors," along with a catechism. In addition to this, Knox taught them from the Gospel of John, but did this in the chapel within the castle at a set hour. As a result of this public teaching, others in the place had an opportunity to notice his teaching ability. John Rough, the man who was doing the work of a preacher for the band, was one of those who noticed Knox's ability, and earnestly asked Knox to take the "preaching place" upon him, but John Knox utterly refused, saying that he would not run where God had not called him. By this he meant that he would do nothing without a lawful calling.

A council adjourned, and those who wanted Knox to preach determined that they would provide that lawful calling. And so John Rough preached a sermon, the sum of which was that a congregation—and a congregation consisted of any which passed the number of two or three—had authority over a man in whom they perceived the gifts of God. And when they called such a one, it was dangerous to refuse to hear the voice of those who desired to be instructed.

Having laid out the points of his sermon, John Rough then turned to make application to John Knox in particular, and publicly issued John Knox's call to the ministry. This call is worth quoting in full:

> *Brother, ye shall not be offended, albeit that I speak unto you that which I have in charge, even from all those that are here present, which is this: In the name of God, and of his Son Jesus Christ, and in the name of these that presently calls you by my mouth, I charge you, that ye refuse not this holy vocation, but that as ye tender the glory of God, the increase of Christ his kingdom, the*

> *edification of your brethren, and the comfort of me,*
> *whom ye understand well enough to be oppressed by*
> *the multitude of labours, that ye take upon you the public*
> *office and charge of preaching, even as ye look to avoid*
> *God's heavy displeasure, and desire that he shall multiply*
> *his graces with you.*[25]

Rough then asked the congregation whether this did not represent their desire. They replied that they approved of the calling. At this point, John Knox hardly fulfills the caricature of "stern reformer" that many have of him. He burst into "most abundant tears," and withdrew to his chamber. From that point to the first time when he appeared to preach in public, Knox was visibly shaken, his countenance showing the "grief and trouble" of his heart. He was, by all accounts, a most reluctant aspirant to the ministry.

The first occasion for this public ministry was not long in coming, however. John Rough was a good man, but relatively unlearned. He was sound in doctrine, but his literary accomplishments were moderate.[26] Knox, by contrast, was thoroughly educated and a formidable debater, but before proceeding we must understand that this was not a modern hostage situation, surrounded with SWAT teams. The Castilians held the castle, but they still had time to come out for theological debates. One papist, a man named Dean John Annand, had greatly troubled John Rough in his preaching, and Knox had helped Rough behind the scenes. Now, John Knox would soon collide with Annand in a public debate in the parish kirk of St. Andrews.

Knox badly mangled Annand's reputation as a result of this debate, which concerned the authority of the church. Annand said what he had to say and then withdrew. Knox then offered himself to prove, in words or writing, that the

Roman church was farther degenerated from the purity of the days of the apostles than the Jews had been when they crucified Christ. This stirred the people greatly, and so they asked John Knox to preach the following Sunday, which he did.

In that sermon, Knox preached with great rhetorical effect, showing that the Roman church was to be considered as the synagogue of Satan. He pulled no punches, and consequently one response to the sermon was that others snipped at the outer "branches of the Papistry; but he strikes at the root to destroy the whole."[27] This was an accurate summary. From his first sermon, John Knox set the pattern for the rest of his life. He was no temporizer.

To have John Knox thundering in the church at St. Andrews caused a problem. The bishop of St. Andrews (not yet consecrated) wrote to the subprior of the church, a man named Winram, wondering why such "heretical and schismatical" doctrines were tolerated there without rebuke. Winram was more than a little friendly to the reformed party, but it would not do to provoke the incoming bishop. He therefore convened a hearing, summoned Knox and Rough, asked a few nominal questions to discharge his responsibilities in the affair, and then turned the remaining questions over to a Greyfriar named Arbuckle. Arbuckle set out to prove the divine authority of the Roman ceremonies, but was soon reduced to the shift of saying that the apostles were not inspired when they wrote the epistles, but were inspired when they established the ceremonies to be handed down. In short, the first verbal battles in the Reformation of Scotland were won by those with Protestant convictions.

However, we must return to our political crisis, because it determines the events that immediately follow. Knox was able to defeat a monk in debate, but was not able to overcome the French military, which was soon to arrive.

The motives of the assassins had been a mix—religious, personal, and political. The fact that John Knox approved of the assassination of the cardinal did not mean that he approved of all the Castilians. Far from it. Knox was not ever one to show partiality. From the first opportunity he had in the public ministry of the Word, he condemned sin everywhere he saw it, and there was plenty inside the castle. His theme to his cohorts was that "their corrupt life could not escape punishment of God."[28] Knox knew that the castle was bound to fall because of the sinfulness of the Castilian band. His views on this were determined by a fixed understanding of Scripture, at the heart of which was his conviction that God is not mocked, and that a man reaps what he sows. When things were going well for the Castilians, and they boasted in it, Knox replied that they did not see what he saw. When they bragged about the thickness of the castle walls, Knox said that the walls were eggshells. Not surprisingly, Knox was proven correct.

A French force arrived by sea, and the castle was assaulted—the battle going badly for the Castilians. Under duress, the Castilians surrendered upon terms. Their lives were to be spared, they were to be transported to France, and forced into the service of the French king. If they did not want to serve him, they were to be conveyed to any country of their choice other than Scotland, but treachery was in the air. Once the prisoners had been taken, they were all shipped off to row in the galleys. And despite Knox's faithfulness, he was taken with them, and set to the oars.[29]

GALLEY SLAVE

*W*ARREN LEWIS, brother of C.S. Lewis, makes the point bluntly. "Until the coming of the concentration camp, the galley held an undisputed pre-eminence as the darkest blot on Western civilization; a galley, said a poetic observer shudderingly, would cast a shadow in the blackest midnight."[30]

Lewis was writing of life in the galleys a century after Knox rowed in them, but from all accounts, the time Knox spent there was a time of horror just as it was for his Huguenot brothers 100 years later.

> *Life on board when the galley was at sea was a sort of Hell's picnic, for there was really no accommodation for anyone. For the convicts, there was, of course, no ques-tion of sleep . . . Cooking facilities were primitive, and, as no one ever washed, the ship crawled with vermin from stem to stern. From below came the constant clank of chains, the crack of whips on bare flesh, screams of*

> *pain, and savage growls. At each oar all five men must*
> *rise as one at each stroke, push the eighteen-feet oar*
> *forward, dip it in the water, and pull with all their force,*
> *dropping into a sitting position at the end of each stroke.*
> *"One would not think", says a Huguenot convict, "that it*
> *was possible to keep it up for half an hour, and yet I have*
> *rowed full out for twenty-four hours without pausing for*
> *a single moment."* [31]

Constant rowing did not bring about the despair of the galley slaves. Had it been, they would all have died in short order. Nevertheless, the whole time, including the respite provided by winter, had to have been the most severe trial. Knox speaks of it as a time of "torment." Years after, he spoke of the "sobs of his heart" and how he was "sore troubled by corporal infirmity."[32] For those who have not experienced such things, all such words should be taken as understatement.

Knox was for two years a *galerien* in the French galleys, a very common and expendable form of cheap fuel. As they were taken away to the galleys, Knox recounts that the "joy of the Papists both of Scotland and France" was at that time in "full perfection." He relates their song of triumph over the Protestants.

> *Preasts content you now; Preasts content you now;*
> *For Normand and his company has filled the galleys*
> *fow [full].* [33]

As prisoners, they could be forced to row for a Roman Catholic power; however, they refused to accommodate themselves to the Roman religion in any way. In his history, Knox relates one representative story of their very Scottish resistance to idolatry. Though in the course of the story Knox does not state it outright, the prisoner involved is probably Knox himself.

Sometimes the Mass was said on the galleys, and sometimes on shore alongside the galleys within the hearing of the slaves. On Saturday nights, the *Salve Regina* was sung, and all the Scots would cover their heads with whatever caps or hoods they had available. On one occasion, after they had arrived at Nantes, the *Salve* was sung, and an idol of Mary they called "Nostre Dame" was presented. The idol was presented to one of the prisoners in chains, and he was required to kiss it. He replied gently, "Trouble me not; such an idol is accursed; and therefore I will not touch it." Instead, his captors responded that he *would* handle it, thrust it into his face, and put it between his hands. Seeing his opportunity, the prisoner threw the idol into the river, and said, "Let our Lady now save herself: she is light enough; let her learn to swim."[34] After this, Knox relates, no Scottish man was urged to participate in that particular form of idolatry.

Knox compared this time in the galleys with the Jewish exile into Babylon. He placed a great importance upon the prisoners keeping themselves pure from idolatry during this time of testing. They were prisoners of *conscience.* In the winter of 1548, a Protestant captive on land named Henry Balnaves had written a treatise on justification by faith. Somehow, he had managed to get it to Knox who, in spite of the circumstances, managed to *edit* it, and write a commendatory epistle. The work, thus revised, was dispatched to Scotland. The irony was not lost on Knox, who spoke of it with a grim humor. He was not oblivious to the oddity of the situation— "incommodity of place, as well as imbecility of mind."[35]

In the summer of 1548, the galleys that contained our prisoners were sitting off the east coast of Scotland. One of

Knox's fellow prisoners pointed to the spires of St. Andrews, and asked Knox if he knew the place. The reply was one of Knox's famous prophecies, which we will discuss later in the book. Knox said, "Yes, I know it well; for I see the steeple of that place where God first opened my mouth in public to his glory; and I am fully persuaded, how weak so ever I now appear, that I shall not depart this life, till that my tongue shall glorify his godly name in the same place."[36] How these words came about, we shall soon see.

During this time, some of the Castilians of greater importance had been taken to prison instead of to the galleys. One of them, William Kirkcaldy, wrote to John Knox, and sought his counsel. The question was whether they could break out of prison in good conscience. Knox's reply to this question is revealing in a number of respects. He said "that if without the blood of any shed or spilt by them for their deliverance, they might set themselves at freedom, that they might safely take it: but to shed any man's blood for their freedom, thereto would he never consent."[37] Far from being a bloodthirsty religious fanatic, Knox was consistently a man of conscience. After receiving the advice, Kirkcaldy and some others escaped successfully—without blood.

John Knox was released from the galleys after nineteen months, and came afterward to England. Although we do not have the details, he was probably released due to negotiations initiated by England, culminating in an exchange of prisoners. As a result, all of the Castilians were released, with the exception of James Melville, the man who had actually killed the cardinal. He had died a natural death before the time of their release.

KNOX THE PURITAN

*A*FTER THE death of Henry VIII in 1547, his son—
Edward VI—who was just a young boy at the
time, inherited the throne. Henry had brought the Reformation to England by breaking with Rome, but did so out of his
desire to obtain his divorce, and not through any genuine
desire for sound or thorough reformation. Consequently,
while the Church of England did separate from the Church
of Rome, the practice of worship in the church remained
largely untouched. Thomas Cranmer, the archbishop of Canterbury, had wanted to pursue reformation more thoroughly,
but he had been hindered in this by Henry, who had placed
himself instead of the pope as the earthly head of the church.
The pope was no longer in control, the monasteries had been
suppressed, and the Bible was available in the vernacular.
However, beyond these basic things, the church in England
remained largely as it had been before.

In this state of affairs, a number of individuals in the
English church wanted to see a more thorough reformation,

which was based upon better principles than those which motivated Henry. Because they wanted to "purify" the church of its remaining popish practices, they became known as Puritans. One of the most important things to note about the Puritan party is that they were reformers, not separatists, and not sectarians. Some of these Puritans were root and branch reformers, like John Knox, while others were more moderate, like Thomas Cranmer or Hugh Latimer. Both kinds of Puritan respected the other group and worked together. While they held distinct views on how fast and far the Reformation should go, they all wanted to do more than had been accomplished thus far.

When Henry died, Cranmer was able to set himself more industriously to the cause of Reformation. Part of his efforts included importing theological talent from the Continent— Peter Martyr, Martin Bucer, Paul Fagius, and Emmanuel Tremellius—and setting them up at Oxford and Cambridge.

John Knox was released from the galleys at just this time. Edward had been on the throne for two years. Coming to England, Knox spent about four years there. Knox's abilities were immediately recognized, and he was appointed to be a preacher in Berwick. On the border with Scotland, it was a military town, which had been known for licentiousness and turmoil. It is important to remember that Knox had been called to the ministry, had reluctantly accepted, and then was almost immediately prevented from discharging any of the work of the ministry. By the time he was freed from the galleys, he was inflamed with a love of the truth, and ready to preach. So he thundered in Berwick for two years, producing a visible change in the manners of the town.

During his time in Berwick, Knox met his future wife, a young woman named Marjory Bowes. She was the fifth daughter of ten; her father was Richard Bowes, a strident Roman

Catholic, while her mother was a Protestant. Sometime prior to June of 1553, Knox and Marjory were pledged to one another. However, because of her father's opposition to the match, they did not get married until 1555 or 1556. The marriage appears to have been a happy one. His wife was a true co-laborer with him in the work of reformation. His mother-in-law, Mrs. Bowes, was a kindly woman, and very devout, but prone to morbid introspection. She lived in a compulsive dread over the possibility of being numbered among the reprobate, and John Knox spent much time trying to help her spiritually.

That region of the country was heavily populated with clergy who were overwhelmingly sympathetic to Rome. A charge was soon brought against Knox, saying that he taught that the sacrifice of the Mass was idolatry, which, as charges go, was quite true. He did teach this, and accordingly a public defense for Knox was arranged in April of 1550 at Newcastle before the bishop of Durham. At his defense, Knox's motto— "Spare no arrows"—was well in evidence. His defense was straight up the middle; he articulated a strong statement of the Puritan stand—"all worshiping, honouring, or service invented by the brain of man in the religion of God, without His own express commandment, is idolatry."[38] His defense completely silenced the bishop and made Knox famous throughout northern England.[39]

During the next year, Knox was assigned to preach at Newcastle, a town to the south of Berwick. In December of 1551, the privy council of King Edward showed their appreciation of Knox by making him one of King Edward's six chaplains. These chaplains were sent about the country as itinerant preachers in an attempt to make up for the defects of the established clergy, which were considerable. Knox immersed himself in the work of this reformation, and found

himself respected well enough as to be consulted by the
reformers at court.

His contribution is visible both in the Second Prayer book
of Edward, and in the Forty-two Articles promulgated the
next year. After the death of Edward, one opponent of the
Reformation complained of how influential Knox had been.
"A runagate Scot did take away the adoration or worshiping
of Christ in the sacrament, by whose procurement that
heresy was put into the last communion book; so much prevailed that one man's authority at that time."[40] As much as
some might hate to admit it, one of the important fathers of
the Church of England was John Knox.

At the same time, Knox knew that the reformation in
England was like the seed in Christ's parable, which sprang
up quickly, because the soil was shallow. Knox had a strong
foreboding about the future of England. He was offered the
bishopric at Rochester, which he declined. While apprecia-
tive of the opportunities for reformation during the reign of
Edward, with more foresight than most, he did not expect it
to last very long at all. As he put it, "What moved me to
refuse (and that with displeasure of all men, even of those
that best loved me) those high promotions that were offered
by him whom God hath taken from us for our offences?
Assuredly the foresight of trouble to come."[41]

Because of his labors in the Anglican church, some have
assumed that Knox's staunch presbyterian convictions must
have come to him later as a result of his time in Geneva, and
that at this time his willingness to work together in harness
with evangelical bishops indicates that his mind was not yet
settled on the question of ecclesiastical government. But this
is not at all accurate. At no time during his work in England
did Knox compromise his principles, which were already well-
defined, and it must be noted that one of these principles was

unity with true brethren, even when he believed those brethren did not see things as clearly as he did.

Shortly after this, Knox was offered a "living" at All Hallows in the city of London, which he declined in similar fashion to the bishopric. This, and his reason for declining, gave some offense. He did not have freedom in his conscience to accept a settled charge in the current unsettled condition of the church. This bothered the privy council, which wanted to know why Knox was not cooperating more with their efforts to use him in the reformation. They summoned Knox to appear before them, and the answer given by Knox was gracious. He first said that he believed he could be of greater use to the church in another setting. But when pressed on the point, he said that a minister had no right, according to the current laws, to keep unworthy applicants from participating in the sacraments—and this was one of the chief points of a minister's office.

In response to questions, he objected as well to the practice of kneeling at the Lord's Supper. There was a sharp collision between Knox and some of the council members. After a long debate, the council informed him that they had no bad design toward him and were sorry that his mind was contrary to the common order. For his part, Knox was sorry the common order was contrary to what Christ had instituted. While differing, they parted in peace, and Knox continued to work with the Anglican reformers until the persecution instituted by Bloody Mary.

FIASCO IN FRANKFURT

*M*UCH TO the dismay of all who were working for reformation in England, King Edward died at the beginning of July 1553. Queen Mary, a thoroughgoing Roman Catholic, was crowned at the end of July. The numerous martyrs who were to give their lives over the course of the next five years began to gather and assemble offstage. When the last history of the church is finally written, those five years will figure largely in it, a strange mixture of horror and glory.

Knox remained in England and continued with his work, traveling and preaching. By November, the parliament had revoked the laws established in the Reformation, and restored Roman Catholic worship. Protestants were told that they were permitted to observe their form of worship until December 20th, at which time they would be treated by the law as heretics.

Of course, Knox had made his enemies, and they were not slow to take advantage of their new opportunity. These

enemies arranged to seize one of Knox's servants as he
carried letters from Knox to his future wife and mother-in-
law, in the hope of finding something with which to charge
Knox. Finally, when it became obvious that he would be
arrested, Knox was prevailed upon to leave England. He was
more than a little reluctant. In a letter to his betrothed and
her mother, he said that his brethren had "partly by admonition, partly by tears, compelled him to obey." He was not sure
that departing England was what he wanted, for he said,
"never could he die in a more honest quarrel."[42] However, at
the end of January, 1554, he wisely procured a vessel which
landed him safely in Dieppe, a port on the Normandy coast.

But Knox was a warhorse being kept from the battle.
Although he was uneasy about the appearances of his choice
to leave, he knew that God would make the matters plain in
His time. As he put it in a letter, "My prayer is, that I may be
restored to the battle again,"[43] and as subsequent events
would prove, Knox was animated with a very great personal
courage. Any questions raised here concerning his courage
were answered in full later.[44]

After about a month, he left Dieppe and traveled through
Switzerland, conversing with the leaders of the Reformation
there. He returned to Dieppe, wrote to his "afflicted
brethren" in England, and then returned to Geneva—where
he met John Calvin. Knox and Calvin soon established an
affectionate friendship, which lasted until Calvin's death in
1564. It was probably during this time that Knox acquired a
mastery of Hebrew, which he had not had opportunity to
learn in his earlier education.

The persecution in England had grown hot, and large
numbers of Protestants had made their way to the Continent. A number of the Reformed cities in Europe arranged
for settlements of Englishmen. One of these was Frankfurt,

a rich imperial city of Germany. Some Protestants came to Frankfurt, and were graciously given a church for worship, which they shared with some French Protestants. The magistrates of the city gave it to the English refugees on the condition that they keep their English worship as close to the French liturgy as possible. This band of refugees wrote to Knox in Geneva and invited him to become one of their pastors, and Knox accepted the responsibility.

Some of the English refugees on the Continent, however, insisted on worshiping according to the Anglican order as established under King Edward. For example, the English in Zurich and Strausburg argued that to change anything now would be an insult to those Anglican martyrs in England who were sealing their testimony with blood. As a result of this, a controversy arose in the church at Frankfurt. After some wrangling, the groups decided to consult with Calvin. Calvin wrote back that he was disappointed that they were quarreling over such a thing, and although he was a moderate on ceremonial issues, he had to condemn those who clung to old customs superstitiously. At the beginning of reformation, Calvin said, the tolerable fooleries (*tolerabiles ineptias*) in the Book of Common Prayer were, well, tolerable, but when God gave opportunity to take the next step, they had an obligation to take that step. There was no necessity to observe the English liturgy in all its details.

Knox, a peaceable man, brokered an agreement between the parties. The agreement was that they would follow the English liturgy as closely as they could, given the circumstances. They would do this until the following April, and if a dispute arose in the meantime, it would be referred to five of the leading ministers in Europe. "The agreement was subscribed by all the members of the congregation; thanks were publicly returned to God for the restoration of harmony; and the communion was received as a pledge of union, and of the burial of all past offenses."[45]

This union was short-lived, however. A fresh company of exiles arrived, led by Richard Cox, a prejudiced man who had been chancellor at Oxford. The newcomers insisted on worshiping in just the way they had done at home, and one of their number took it upon himself to enter the pulpit and read the litany. Knox said nothing at the time, but in the afternoon service, he admonished those through whom a "godly agreement" was "ungodly broken." The new arrivals constituted an obstinate majority, but a magistrate of the city quickly blocked them. He warned the congregation that the use of the church was only permissible under certain conditions, and that if they did not meet those conditions, he would close the doors.

The new arrivals seemed bent on making trouble and accused Knox of treason to the Frankfurt magistracy. In a work published the previous July, Knox had mentioned in passing that the Emperor Charles V was "no less an enemy to Christ than ever was Nero." This put the magistrates of Frankfurt in a bind. Knox was the leader of the group who had faithfully worked with their directions. On the other hand, Charles was at that time in Augsburg—within 160 miles of Frankfurt. The leaders of the city asked Knox if he would relieve them from their difficult situation by voluntarily stepping down. This Knox did, followed by other faithful Christians from that church.

Far from wrecking the church, Knox was the man who kept it together as long as could be done in an impossible situation. Not surprisingly, given the temper and demeanor of those who destroyed the work there, the church did not fare well after they forced the Puritans to go and was wracked with ongoing dissension.

Even after the fact, both parties were interested in gaining the judgment of Calvin to support their side. Though Calvin's doctrinal sympathies were closer to the Puritans, he was not really interested in singing psalms to a dead horse. Nevertheless, Calvin *was* willing to say one thing, which serves as a fitting conclusion to this unhappy chapter. "I cannot keep secret, that Master Knox was, in my judgment, neither godly nor brotherly dealt withal."[46]

First Visit Back to Scotland

*A*FTER THE fall of the Castle at St. Andrews, the fortunes of the Protestants in Scotland had fallen markedly. Several factors conspired, however, over the course of the following years, to bring about a rising tide of reformational sentiment.

The earl of Arran became regent of Scotland after the death of James V. The wife of James, Mary of Guise, the queen dowager, had long wanted to get the power of the regency for herself, and, after much court intrigue, she finally succeeded in April of 1554. Part of her "campaigning" had included some favor (for political reasons only) shown to the Protestants.

In the meantime, Mary of England made contributions of her own. First, she had married Philip, king of Spain, and Spain was a great rival to France. Mary, the queen-regent of Scotland, held close attachments to France. It is not surprising that the two women did not get along, and soon there was an open breach between them. Further, Mary of England was Bloody Mary, and her fierce persecution of Protestants had led some of them to flee to Scotland. Under the queen-regent in Scotland they were left alone, and even permitted to teach in private.

The *need* for ecclesiastical reformation continued in Scotland as well. The corruption in the Church was massive, and even drew the attention of several Church councils. One council met in Edinburgh in 1549, and acknowledged that "corruption and profane lewdness of life, as well as gross ignorance of arts and sciences, reigned among the clergy of almost every degree."[47] The council issued fifty-eight canons intended to address the evils, but unfortunately, the authority to correct the Church was held by those who needed correction themselves, and effective reformation from within the establishment was consequently impossible. This meant that the clergy by their lives continued to alienate the Scottish populace.

Knox, who had been separated from his betrothed for about two years and was anxious to see her, sailed from Dieppe and landed near the border of Scotland and England. He went from there to Berwick in August of 1555, where he found his future wife and her mother in a good situation, meeting with a small band of Christians who had stayed faithful during the persecutions of Mary.

He traveled secretly to Edinburgh and began to teach. Before too much was done in preaching, Knox was anxious to have a practical evil remedied. Most of the Protestants at this time still attended Mass, holding it to be an imperfect form of worship rather than a positive sin. John Knox and a temporizing Protestant, William Maitland, were the two principal debaters at a private conference held in Edinburgh to address the question. It was determined at the council that Knox's position had prevailed, and that Protestants should begin meeting separately, as Reformed congregations, with separate communion. It would be hard to overestimate the importance of this event. If there were any particular event that can be identified as the formal start of the Scottish Reformation, it would be this one. This council declared and sacramentally sealed a formal corporate separation from the established Church at this time.

This issue settled, Knox began to travel widely, teaching and administering the Lord's Supper in houses. "That knave Knox," as one of the bishops called him, was entirely too successful in this ministry, and so was summoned to appear before the authorities. While Knox was staying at the house of Erskine of Dun, he received a summons to appear at a trial "before an ecclesiastical court at Blackfriars' Church in Edinburgh" on the 15th of May.[48] Such citations were commonly used as a signal to the offender that it was time to make tracks for the tall grass, but much to the embarrassment and chagrin of the ecclesiastical authorities, Knox showed up for his trial. The clergy were unsure of the queen-regent's support, and so they canceled the trial on a technicality, and made themselves scarce.

Knox took the opportunity thus presented to him, and preached on the day his trial was to have been, and did so in a large lodging belonging to the bishop of Dunkeld. He did this for ten days following, morning and afternoon, and no one attempted to stop him. What began as an authoritative threat turned into a disaster for the clergy.

It was at this time that Knox was asked to write a letter to the queen-regent. Knox wrote the letter with great care, and although he was a plainspoken man, his style was not inelegant or maladroit. "Superfluous and foolish it shall appear to many, that I, a man of base estate and condition, dare enterprise to admonish a princess so honourable, endued with wisdom and singular graces."[49] In the letter, he called upon the queen-regent to do whatever she could to further the cause of reformation in Scotland. Although he honored her office and position, he was faithful to his charge and did not mince words.

> *Unless in your regiment, and in using of power, your*
> *grace is found different from the multitude of princes*
> *and head rulers, that this preeminence wherein you are*
> *placed shall be your dejection to torment and pain ever-*
> *lasting. This proposition is sore, but, alas! it is so true,*
> *that if I should conceal and hide it from your grace,*
> *I committed no less treason against your grace, than*
> *if I did see you by imprudency take a cup which I knew*
> *to be poisoned or envenomed, and yet would not*
> *admonish you to abstain from drinking of the same.* [50]

The queen-regent was not impressed when she received the letter. She looked it over carelessly, and handed it to the archbishop of Glasgow, saying, "Please you, my lord, to read a pasquil."[51] A pasquil was a satire. She did not take his letter seriously at all, so later in 1558, when Knox was back on the Continent, he sent her a revised version that drove the arguments home with even greater force. He was serious, and the issues involved could not be so easily dismissed. He desired no armor in his battle with the papists other than "Goddis holie word, and the libertie of my tonge."[52]

While Knox was engaged in this formational work in Scotland, he received news that the English Congregation in Geneva had called him to become their pastor. He resolved to obey this summons, and made preparations to leave. Marjory and Mrs. Bowes were with him in Edinburgh by this time. Because Mrs. Bowes was now a widow, she was able to go to Europe with them. Knox sent them on ahead to Dieppe, and took a last tour of the places he had been preaching. Then, in July of 1556, he left the country, joined Marjory and Mrs. Bowes in Dieppe, and traveled with them to Geneva.

As soon as the clergy understood that he had left the country, they immediately renewed the summons against him. When he failed to appear, they condemned him "adjudging his body to the flames, and his soul to damnation"[53] and consequently burned him in effigy at the cross of Edinburgh. The cat left and the mice had a trial.

KNOX THE HUGUENOT

*T*O SAY that Knox had a profound effect on the history of his native country would be an understatement. If the name of Knox is recognized at all, it is associated with Scotland. Those who are a little more familiar with his life must also acknowledge his contributions to the formation of Puritanism in the Church of England. In addition to his years in England, he was also the pastor of the English congregation in Geneva—the congregation that produced the famous Geneva Bible and a metrical Psalter in English. That particular congregation of expatriates was small, but had a profound impact on the subsequent course of events in England.

However, very few recognize the role that Knox played in the Reformation in France. There are several reasons for this, the first being that the later persecution of the French Huguenots or Protestants was "successful" in the sense that it either drove them from the country, or brought upon them the glory of martyrdom. The Protestant movement in France was initially quite a vigorous one, but unfortunately was not ordained to remain a permanent force there. The persecutions of the seventeenth century drove the Huguenots to America, to South Africa, and many thousands of them to Heaven.

One Huguenot on his way to the galleys wrote to his wife—"we lie fifty-three of us in a place which is not about thirty feet in length and nine in breadth . . . There is scarce one of us who does not envy the condition of several dogs and horses," and as Warren Lewis mentions, this Huguenot's conclusion to his letter is worthy to be written in letters of gold. "When I reflect on the merciful providence of God towards me, I am ravished with admiration and do evidently discover the secret steps of Providence which hath formed me from my youth after a requisite manner to bear what I suffer."[54] John Piper tells the story of a young Huguenot girl, fourteen years old, who was brought before the authorities and required to renounce her faith by simply saying *j'abjure.* She refused to comply, and together with thirty other women, was confined in a tower by the sea. She continued there for the next thirty-eight years, and instead of *j'abjure,* she, with her fellow prisoners, scratched one word on the stone wall—*resistez.*[55] The story of the Huguenots has not been adequately told, and cannot really be until the last day reveals the secrets of men.

During the time that God allowed Protestantism to thrive in France, however, it was indebted in part to the service of John Knox, but this is not widely recognized because Knox's contribution was made "on the run" or "by the way." Put in modern terms, Knox carried on an effective ministry during his time in airports. As we have seen a number of times already, Knox passed through Dieppe repeatedly, on the French coast, either to board a ship, or to send or receive communications from England or Scotland, and it is here that we see his influence.

After the first visit of Knox to Dieppe, a Genevan merchant named Jean Venable used his influence to form a Reformed congregation. In the early years, the small church met at night in houses and in cellars. The church had a pastor, but Knox was present for some of this time. He spoke French fluently and may have been of some help in the preaching and teaching— although his literary work occupied most of his time.

The last time Knox came through Dieppe, he spent ten weeks there. The little church there had had different pastors over time, but had always met at night. During Knox's short ministry there in 1559, the number of the faithful had increased to the point where they were able to preach the Word in broad daylight. From this distance, it is hard to tell whether the increase of the Protestant numbers made the openness possible, or whether Knox's dislike of skulking was the kind of boldness that attracted men and women to the new teaching. Did numbers lead to boldness, or boldness to numbers? Perhaps it was a combination of both. In any case, a great blessing in growth came to this congregation.

Shortly before Knox left this congregation, a member of the congregation wrote to Calvin, requesting a minister to labor in the wake of Knox. He based the request on the remarkable success of "Master John Knox, a singular instrument of the Holy Spirit, who, according to the graces bountifully poured out upon him by the Lord, has faithfully promoted, by his preaching, the glory of Christ, during the short time that it has been in his power to have fellowship with us."[56]

A month after Knox had to leave them, the congregation celebrated the Lord's Supper. Between six and eight hundred people participated, including the governor of the castle and some of the leading citizens of the town. Knox continued correspondence with the church there. Between 1625 and

1630, the number of the Protestants there had grown to over 5,000.[57]

Incidentally, in this wayside ministry we see that Knox was certainly no political bigot. Elsewhere we learn that Knox was unalterably opposed to the political alliance that existed at this time between Scotland and France. Remember, also, that he had rowed in the French galleys for nineteen months, but his ministry among Frenchmen shows him a true servant of the gospel and covenant, and not one driven by partisan "patriotic" interests.

RETURN TO SCOTLAND

*J*OHN KNOX returned to Scotland on May 2, 1559. He preached at Dundee, and then afterward at Perth, to great effect.[58] Word came to the authorities that he was back, and within a few days he was declared an outlaw because of the previous sentence that had been passed against him.

Providentially, it was at just this time that the queen-regent had summoned certain Protestant preachers for trial at Stirling by usurping the ministerial office and for administering the Lord's Supper in a different manner than the Catholic Church acknowledged. There were four preachers summoned to appear—Paul Methven, John Christison, William Harlaw, and John Willock. Several of the Protestant leaders protested to the queen against these proceedings. The queen replied haughtily that in spite of them, "all their preachers should be banished from Scotland." When they reminded her of the promises she had previously made to protect them, she replied in a manner common to those in power—that it "became not subjects to burden their princes with promises, farther than they pleased to keep them."[59]

The day after he landed in Scotland, Knox wrote in a letter that he saw that "the battle shall be great . . . For my fellow-preachers have a day appointed to answer before the queen-regent . . . when I intend also to be present."[60] As Knox traveled toward Stirling with the indicted preachers, a great but unarmed multitude assembled around them. They stopped at Perth, and sent word ahead to Stirling so that the authorities knew they were coming in peace. This concerned the queen-regent, and so she sent word that the preachers did not have to appear. This pleased the Protestants greatly, and so they for the most part returned to their homes. However, when the day of trial came and the preachers failed to appear, their judges condemned them as outlaws.

The room was filled with gasoline fumes. It only remained for a match to be struck. Knox had remained in Perth, and on the day the news of this breach of the queen-regent's promise came, he preached immediately on the idolatry of the Mass. After the sermon, Knox dismissed the congregation and only a few remained behind. A priest, perhaps lacking in prudence, uncovered an altar and prepared to say Mass in the church. A boy standing nearby expressed his disapproval, and the priest struck him. The boy retaliated by throwing a stone at the priest, which struck and broke one of the images on the altar. At this, the riot was on. A mob quickly gathered, and not finding sufficient employment at the church, headed for the monasteries.

The preachers and magistrates, as soon as they heard of the riot, gathered, and, despite all their efforts, were unable to restrain the mob. The houses of the black and grey friars were soon laid level to the ground. Knox called the tumult the work of "the rascal multitude." Far from being an instigator, Knox gave himself heartily to the work of restraining the people. As much as he wanted to destroy all idolatry, he wanted it done according to law, decently and in order.

Knox knew that Mary, the queen-regent, would use this turmoil against him, and he was right. The queen-regent assembled an army, vowing to lay waste to the town, and the citizens of the city prepared to defend themselves. Because they were ready to fight, the queen-regent negotiated a settlement, to which the inhabitants of Perth readily agreed, but once the queen-regent occupied the town, she broke the terms of the agreement. Due to this treachery, the noblemen who adhered to the Protestant faith came together and established a covenant, and began at this time to be known as the Lords of the Congregation. Her behavior here lost her the support of the powerful Lord James Stuart, later to become regent of Scotland. The lords established the reformed faith in those places of Scotland where their authority extended.

Knox had arrived in Scotland in the midst of considerable turmoil. He resolved to preach at St. Andrews, despite the threat of the bishop to receive him with a twelve-gun salute, the "most part of which would light upon his nose."[61] The noblemen accompanying Knox urged him to refrain from trying to preach there, at least for the time being. Knox, who had a true leader's instinct for timing, refused. He had predicted, while still in the galleys, that he would preach in St. Andrews, and here was the opportunity. As for safety, he said, "My life is in the custody of Him whose glory I seek. I desire the hand nor weapon of no man to defend me. I only crave audience; which, if it be denied here unto me at this time, I must seek where I may have it."[62] Having made this resolve, Knox preached on the expulsion of the money changers from the Temple of God, and was able to preach without incident or interruption.

While the Lords of the Congregation and the queen-regent were in a military standoff, the work of Reformation in Scotland began to grow. The queen-regent was seeking help from France, and the Congregation was negotiating with the government of Elizabeth I in England, seeking aid from that quarter.

By October, the Lords of the Congregation determined to suspend the queen-regent from her office, but they did so with three stipulations. First, they did not understand their action as releasing them from their due allegiance to their sovereigns in France, Mary Queen of Scots and her new husband, Francis. Secondly, they were motivated by their concern for the safety of the commonwealth, and not by any animosity toward Mary of Guise. Thirdly, their action did not preclude the restoration of the queen-regent to her office if she exhibited sorrow for her behavior and showed an inclination to submit to the advice of the estates of the realm.[63]

This dramatic step taken, the fortunes of the Protestants drastically worsened. A series of military and financial setbacks greatly distressed them, and the army of the Congregation retreated, despondent, to Stirling. Only Knox was unsubdued. The day after the army arrived in Stirling, Knox entered the pulpit, and literally preached an army back to life, but he did not do this by preaching about the sins of the enemy; he set forth, in plain language, the sins of the Congregation. As McCrie points out, the "audience, who had entered the church in deep despondency, left it with renovated courage."[64] A council met that afternoon and dispatched a messenger to the English court, who was finally successful, in February of 1560, in contracting a formal treaty between Elizabeth and the Lords of the Congregation. By April, an English army joined the forces of the Congregation, which forced the French back to the city of Leith. At just this critical time, the queen-regent, in deteriorating health, went to the castle at Edinburgh, where she died during the siege of Leith.

Because Elizabeth had finally entered the conflict with some vigor, the French granted her demands and a treaty was signed on the 7th of July. According to the terms of the treaty, a council would determine the affairs of state in Scotland— chosen in part by Francis and Mary, and in part by the estates of Scotland. The English army returned to England, leaving behind Scottish gratitude—a remarkable conclusion in itself to a remarkable twelve months.

MARY QUEEN OF SCOTS

*B*Y ANY reckoning, Mary Queen of Scots remains a fascinating character. One of John Knox's great misfortunes, one that certainly damaged his reputation with many, was the ability that he had to see through her. As Otto Scott put it, "John Knox was the only man who ever met Mary Stuart who was neither charmed nor deceived."[65] Mary *was* charming, beautiful, intelligent, witty . . . and amoral. Knox was principled, blunt, and honest. A collision was inevitable, and it occurred as soon as Mary returned to Scotland from France.

Mary was the lawful heir of the throne of Scotland, and her claim acknowledged by all, including Knox. At the conclusion of the civil war, the Protestants were firmly in power, and the Reformation well established in Scotland. Mary was adamantly opposed to the Reformation, having been brought up in the court of France, a major Catholic power. Given the situation, it is astounding that the Scots invited her to return home. A reverse situation—a Protestant queen invited to rule a Catholic power—was inconceivable, and the decision to call Mary was really an amazing demonstration of devotion to biblical principle.

When the nobles invited Mary to return to Scotland, they could not promise her anything concerning her religion more than the private exercise of it. But Mary was not accustomed to being crossed, and urged on by her advisors, she directed that preparations be made to observe the Mass at Holyrood House on the first Lord's Day after her arrival. This Mass was said, not only for Mary, but also for her uncles and her French entourage.

The following Sunday John Knox declared from the pulpit of St. Giles that one Mass was more fearful to him than 10,000 men "landed in any part of the realm, of purpose to suppress the whole religion."[66] A few days later, the queen summoned John Knox to appear before her. She accused him of three things—the first being that he raised the subjects of Scotland against her mother. Secondly, she accused him of having written a book against her lawful authority. That book was the *Monstrous Regiment of Women,* written during the reign of Bloody Mary. The last accusation was her suggestion that he was as powerful as he was because of an employment of magical arts.

According to one source, John Knox was five feet two inches tall, while another records Mary as at least six feet tall. However, little is much when placed in the hands of God. John Knox was much for God.

Knox answered her objections carefully, and at the conclusion of the interview, Knox said, "I pray God, madam, that you may be as blessed within the commonwealth of Scotland, as ever Deborah was in the commonwealth of Israel."[67] Although Knox spoke to her plainly, and in a manner that was novel to her, he did not address her with any rudeness or disrespect. He was certainly not a creature of the court; "But what did you go out to see? A man clothed in soft garments? Indeed, those who wear soft clothing are in kings' houses (Matthew 11:8)." One doctrine articulated by Knox in this interview is important because of its later implications, and applications. "If princes exceed their bounds, and do against that wherefore they should be obeyed, there is no doubt that they may be resisted even with power."[68] As heirs of the American War for Independence, it is a principle we should understand better than we do.

Her second interview with Knox, in December of 1562, was occasioned by another sermon in which Knox had referred to princes who "were more exercised in dancing and music than in reading or hearing the word of God, and delight more in fiddlers and flatterers than in the company of wise and grave men."[69] Knox delivered this sermon after a splendid ball held at the palace—with dancing to a late hour. At first glance, it appears that Knox was insulting the court for no other reason than that he was being the sixteenth-century equivalent of a stuffed shirt. But the problem with this simple explanation is that the ball was thrown after Mary had received a report from France concerning successful persecution against the Huguenots. The persecution had been inaugurated with an attack conducted by her uncles on a congregation of French Huguenots in a massacre at Vassy. That congregation had been peaceably assembled when they were assaulted by an armed force killing and wounding a number of them, women and children included. In his sermon, Knox allowed that dancing was certainly lawful, "provided those who practised it did not neglect the duties of their station, and did not dance, like the

Philistines, from joy at the misfortunes of God's people."[70]
Mary heard a distorted account of the sermon, and summoned
Knox. He repeated what he had said, and those who had heard
him verified that he summarized the sermon well.

The third interview went tolerably well. The preceding
Easter, Mass had been celebrated in various places. When the
law against this was not enforced, a few ardent Protestants
arrested some priests, and declared that they would enforce
the law. Mary summoned Knox to enlist his aid in suppress-
ing such vigilantism, but Knox pointed to the example of
Phineas in the Old Testament, and told the queen that the
way out of the impasse was for *her* to enforce the law. She
did not receive this counsel in a good temper, but then
changed her mind and told Knox the next day that she would
have the offending priests tried.

The next encounter was probably the most unpleasant.
Knox had referred in a sermon to a rumor that the queen
was considering marriage to Don Carlos of Spain. Don
Carlos was the son of Philip II of Spain, who was an arch-
persecutor of Protestants. Knox had said that if the nobility
of Scotland consented to have an infidel become head of
their sovereign, they would "bring God's vengeance upon
the country."[71] To Mary, this comment by Knox appeared to
be the pinnacle of meddlesomeness. When Knox was ush-
ered into her presence, the queen was in a "vehement
fume," and amid threats and tears, demanded, "What have
ye to do with my marriage, and who are ye within this
commonwealth?"[72] Knox replied that although he was not
among the nobility, God had made him a profitable member
within the commonwealth, and that he had a duty to speak
out when the nation was threatened. Mary responded pas-
sionately, and with more tears. Knox, apparently touched,
said that he did not delight in the weeping of any of God's

creatures, and that he had difficulty with the weeping of his boys when he disciplined them.

He was asked to step out to the antechamber to await the queen's pleasure. While there he spoke with the fair ladies of the court assembled there about the transitory nature of all earthly things.

With the exception of Lord Ochiltree, all Knox's friends at court were afraid to show him the slightest countenance, because it looked bad for Knox. But he pressed on, "O fair ladies, how plesing war this lyfe of yours, if it sould ever abyde, and then, in the end, that we might pas to hevin with all this gay gear! But fye upon that knave Death, that will come whidder we will or not."[73] In a mixture of serious exhortation and joking banter, the Reformer occupied himself with conversation until he was told that he was dismissed until the queen had taken further advice.

The last occasion where the queen and Knox met was of a semi-public nature, and that was at John Knox's trial for treason. In the summer of 1563, the arrangement that the Mass would be said only in the queen's presence was violated. The queen was absent from Edinburgh, and two zealous Protestants—Patrick Cranstoun and Andrew Armstrong—openly protested at one of the celebrations of the Mass. They were cited to appear for trial, and Knox wrote a letter to the brethren asking for their presence, comfort, and assistance at the trial. Mary saw a copy of Knox's letter and accused Knox of treason, because he (allegedly) had tried to assemble the queen's lieges. But when the time for Knox's trial came, he had no difficulty in showing that what he had done was perfectly legal, and that he was not treasonous in letter or spirit. The trial ended disastrously for the queen, with Knox acquitted by almost all the members of the Council, including even a personal enemy, the bishop of Ross.

KNOX THE PRESBYTERIAN

*H*OWEVER, NOW we must backtrack for a moment. Knox had arrived back in Scotland in 1559. His wife Marjory died shortly after this in 1560, leaving him with two small boys. The loss devastated him; his wife had been a loyal worker in the cause of Reformation, and a very great help to him. Mary Queen of Scots arrived from France in 1561, and the interviews with the queen we discussed in the previous chapter occurred between 1561 and 1563.

In 1564, Knox further antagonized the queen by marrying again. His second wife was Margaret Stuart, the seventeen-year-old daughter of Lord Ochiltree. This union incensed the queen, but not over their disparity of age. Knox was in his late forties by this time, but the real problem was that the queen did not like the fact that Knox had married into any relationship, however remote, with the royal family. Margaret was a Stuart, and the English ambassador reported that Queen Mary "stormeth wonderfully; for that she [Margaret Stuart] is of the blood and name."[74] We do not know much about

Margaret's married life with Knox other than her ministrations to him on his deathbed, and the fact that she bore him three daughters. The young bride seemed warmly attached to her husband, and we have every reason to believe the marriage was a happy one.

Concurrent with all this activity, Knox was deeply involved in laying the foundations of Scottish Presbyterianism. There were two aspects to this—the first being the adoption of the Confession. After the queen-regent had died, Knox and some collaborators, all with the name of John, drew up a Confession of Faith in response to a request from the Scottish Parliament. "Over the next four days, the Scottish Confession was drafted by six ministers: John Winram, John Spottiswoode, John Willock, John Douglas, John Row, and John Knox. On 17 August 1560, the document was read twice, article by article, before the Parliament; and the Protestant ministers stood ready to defend the cause of truth, in the event that any article of belief was assailed."[75]

The Confession was not the work of theology wonks in a detached and disinterested theological debating society. "For God we take to record in our consciences, that from our hearts we abhor all sects of heresy, and all teachers of erroneous doctrine; and that, with all humility, we embrace the purity of Christ's evangel, which is the only food of our souls; and therefore so precious unto us, that we are determined to suffer the extremity of worldly danger, rather than that we will suffer ourselves to be defrauded of the same."[76] There was some debate over whether or not the Parliament had the legal right, according to the recent treaty, to adopt the Confession without consultations with Queen Mary in France. In the end, those who argued that they did have the independent authority won, and the thoroughly Protestant Confession was adopted.

The Book of Discipline did not have such a smooth road. Just as faith requires works as a testimony, so confessions of faith without governmental applications will always falter. The problem here was the usual one—money. Prior to the Reformation, fully half the wealth of Scotland was in the hands of the established church. Now the Book of Discipline was a proposal for church organization and government, which included the idea that the Catholic church turn over all the lands it owned to the Reformed church. Not surprisingly, the proposal was displeasing to the nobility of Scotland. They had not really had much to lose with the ratification of the Confession, but the Book of Discipline was a different bowl of haggis. This was a great economic threat to the Scottish aristocracy, and so they successfully defeated the Book of Discipline.

One could argue that to change the title of ownership from Catholic to Reformed should have distressed no one, but this would only be the case if the change was in name only. The Book of Discipline proposed that the funds of the Church should actually start going to the work of the Church. In other words, the earlier system included numerous kickbacks, and the aristocracy could easily exploit this system to their own benefit. This proposal, instead, suggested that the Church spend this revenue on the support of ministers, the relief of the poor, and the establishment of schools. In other words, the change would be a true change, and the change would bite.

Those who drafted the Book of Discipline knew that it would be hard to swallow, and acknowledged this in the section on the "Rents and Patrimony of the Kirk." As they put it, "But before we enter in this head, we must crave of your honours, in the name of the eternal God, and of his Son Christ Jesus, that ye have respect to your poor brethren, the labourers and manurers of the ground; who by these cruel beasts, the Papists, have been so oppressed that their life to them has been dolorous and bitter. If ye will have God author and approver of your reformation, ye must not follow their footsteps; but ye must have compassion upon your brethren, appointing them to pay so reasonable teinds [tithes], that they may feel some benefit of Christ Jesus now preached unto them."[77]

The aristocracy rejected this proposal but provided some measure of support for the Church of Scotland—with ecclesiastical revenues divided into three parts. The ejected popish clergy received two thirds of the revenue, with the third part divided between the court and the Protestant ministry. Knox was not happy with the arrangement at all. "I sie twa pairtis freely gevin to the devill, and the third mon be devyded betwix God and the devill."[78] Some have taken the clear economic self-interest exhibited here by the Protestant lords as a basis for calling the entire legitimacy of the Reformation in Scotland into question. Certainly, showcased here is the behavior of a number of fair-weather Protestants, but we must also remember that more than a few noblemen had risked all they had for the sake of reformation. We must also remember that the ministers remained steadfast throughout.

But even though the Book of Discipline was not ratified in the civil realm, the Church of Scotland did ratify the form of government found in the Book of Discipline, as well as some other measures contained there. Knox addressed the General Assembly of the Church of Scotland, and exhorted them to faithfulness in the work of planting the church, and then to entrust the results to the hands of God.[79] At the very beginning of the Scottish Presbyterian Church, the necessity of maintaining a godly independence from the state was made evident. The Church was not only to stand separately when the civil authority was Catholic, the same was necessary even when the civil authorities were fellow Protestants.

ADULTERY AND MURDER AT COURT

*I*N ORDER to understand the next series of events, we have to become better acquainted with some of the figures surrounding the court of Mary. Her half brother, James Stuart, the earl of Moray, was a staunch Protestant. Somewhat rare in the annals of politics, he was an honest man. He was the one who had convinced the Lords of the Congregation that they should invite Mary to take the throne in Scotland. At the same time, he had given his word to Knox and the Lords of the Congregation that he would not permit Mary to overturn the accomplishments of the Reformation. In keeping that promise, he had his hands more than full.

After many false starts and alarms, Mary settled on a second marriage to Henry Stuart, the Lord Darnley. On July 29, 1565, the two were married. Darnley was related to the royal houses of both England and Scotland, and this ensured that if Elizabeth I of England died childless, any child of Mary Queen of Scots would assume the throne of England. This is in fact what happened when her son,

James VI of Scotland, became James I of England. In the matrimonial politics leading up to this surprise, Elizabeth had been outmaneuvered, and she was furious.

The union was a true celebrity union. Darnley was tall, blond, and well-proportioned. Mary herself was at least six feet tall, and was a fascinating, beautiful, and alluring character. It was the sixteenth century, true, but these two were among the *glitterati.* Moray opposed the union, and was driven from the court. He tried to raise an army, crying that the Reform was in danger, but response was lukewarm—only Knox agreed with him. Hardly anyone rallied to his cause, and Moray had to flee to England.

Mary summoned Patrick Hepburn, earl of Bothwell and a great enemy of Moray, back from semi-exile abroad. "Bothwell, with his deep-set eyes, chestnut hair, and simian features, was a fighting machine adored by women and detested by men. 'An ape in purple,' said the poet George Buchanan in one of his unforgettable phrases."[80] Bothwell here enters our story, and Mary's bedchamber, shortly thereafter.

David Rizzio was the queen's secretary and a loathsome man. He was widely disliked in Scotland, more because he was an Italian Roman Catholic than because of the policies he advocated. He exerted an enormous influence at court.

The marriage between Darnley and Mary, like so many marriages of the "beautiful people," was soon in difficulty. Mary had grown quickly tired of him, and he turned increasingly to drink and the comfort provided by the brothels. His behavior was increasingly erratic, and, in short, he was becoming a major embarrassment at court. At around the same time, Darnley had heard rumors, and believed them, that Mary was sleeping with Rizzio. Darnley's jealousy made it easy for some Protestant lords to approach him and begin to hatch a plot against Rizzio's life.

However, this meant that two plots were gestating simultaneously. One, orchestrated through Rizzio, was to restore papal authority in Scotland; the other was to kill Rizzio. This latter plot was executed before the former, and reduced the former to shambles. Darnley, in the grip of his jealousy, wanted Rizzio assassinated in front of the queen, well advanced in her pregnancy. Consequently, one evening, the assassins seized and struck Rizzio in the queen's presence, and dragged him away screaming. "In the large reception room on the landing, they stabbed and slashed at him in a frenzy of hate; one ran and opened the casement window. Finally, slipping in puddles of his blood, they picked him up and threw his still-warm cadaver out into the courtyard below, where it landed with a sickening smack. He had, in the grim phrase of the time, been *Scotched*."[81]

We have no reason to believe that Knox was involved in the plot in any way, as the personal hatred and animosity involved being utterly inconsistent with his character. However, the assassination did alter the political landscape considerably, and Knox was gratified in the resultant change that came to the kingdom. Moray also was able to return from exile, and the queen had to pretend a reconciliation with Darnley and bide her time, but her animosity against her husband was sealed forever, and waited only an opportunity to burst into the open.

When James was born, the event of his baptism was celebrated with great festivities. Absent from all of them—the banquets, dances, the baptism itself—was the young prince's father. In December of 1566, Darnley left the palace early in the morning and retired to his father's seat in Glasgow. "By the time he arrived, the true reason he had not appeared in public was horribly evident. He was lifted from his horse in a state of collapse. His whole body and face had erupted in 'evil favored pistules'—the final and most fearful stage of syphilis."[82]

In the meantime, the queen was sleeping with Bothwell, and the two of them were plotting to get rid of the king. At his bedside, the queen convinced Darnley that he should move back to Edinburgh, and their entourage made its way slowly back to an isolated location at Kirk o' Field. At two o'clock in the morning, after the queen had left him, a tremendous explosion blew apart the wing of the house where Darnley was sleeping. The king killed, suspicion fell on Bothwell almost immediately. Posters—a grand new weapon in this age of printing—began to appear, making this point. The queen was of course a suspected accomplice. The later discovery of sonnets and letters between Mary and Bothwell confirmed the public suspicion.

Behind the scenes, Bothwell became the king of Scotland *de facto,* and decided to brazen the thing out by raping the queen. As she was traveling once with her entourage, Bothwell met her with a thousand men, and took her "forcibly" away. The queen had to marry him now, because he had "ravished her and lain with her against her will."[83]

For those readers who are still with us, in the middle of all this, Bothwell's wife had sued him for divorce because of his adultery with a maid. If this suit were successful, it would mean that according to canon law, Bothwell could not remarry. So he had a pliable churchman make the happy discovery that he and wife, Lady Jean Gordon, were fourth cousins, and that their marriage was invalid to begin with. The queen married Bothwell on the 15th of May—a little over three months from the time of Darnley's murder and twelve days after the groom's divorce. Needless to say, the nation, Protestant and Catholic, was revolted, and so they revolted. "The events which followed in rapid succession upon this infamous marriage—the confederation of the nobility for revenging the king's death, and preserving the person of the infant prince; the flight of Bothwell; the surrender and imprisonment of Mary; her resignation of the government; the coronation of her son; and the appointment of the earl of Moray as regent during his minority, are all well known to the readers of Scottish history."[84]

LATTER MINISTRY AND DEATH

*I*N 1568, Mary escaped from her imprisonment and gathered an army, which was quickly defeated at the battle of Langside. She then fled, and Elizabeth of England subsequently captured and imprisoned her. Kept there for almost twenty years, Elizabeth finally had her executed. While in prison, she remained a formidable political force, skewing the politics of Scotland for years.

At the beginning of this chain of events, John Knox had returned from England, where he had been visiting his sons, and arrived in time to preach the coronation sermon for the young James. While Knox longed for peace, the last four years of his life remained as eventful and tumultuous as the rest of his life had been. For example, a great blow to the Protestant cause came when a young man named James Hamilton assassinated the Regent Moray in January of 1570. Hamilton was one of a group of prisoners captured after the battle at Langside, and, due to be executed, he was "pardoned at the request of Mr. Knox whereof he sore repented."[85] In Knox's sermon that day, he said of Moray, one of the few noblemen whose character he respected, "He is at rest, O Lord; we are left in extreme misery."[86]

As the end of his life approached, Knox's strength was failing, but, for a time, when he came to the pulpit, it would revive. One account of this, made by a young student named James Melville, is worth recounting at length.

> *In the opening up of his text, he was moderat the space of an half houre; but when he entered to application, he made me so to grew [thrill] and tremble, that I could not hald a pen to wryt. He was very weik. I saw him, every day of his doctrine, go hulie and fear [slowly and warily], with a furring of marticks about his neck, a staffe in the ane hand, and gude, godlie Richart Ballenden, his servand, halden up the uther oxter [armpit], from the abbey to the parish kirk, and, by the said Richart, and another servand, lifted up to the pulpit, whar he behovit to lean at his first entrie; bot, er he haid done with his sermone, he was sa active and vigorous, that he was lyk to ding the pulpit in blads, and flie out of it.* [87]

His body was like that pulpit—it had been dinged to blads. He was still relatively young, but life had worn him down. As the end of his life neared, he knew and understood the approach of death. Death came to a contented man. One day two of Knox's close friends came to visit him, and, seeing him to be very sick, they decided they should leave, but he prevailed upon them to stay for dinner, and he got up from bed for the last time. "He ordered a hogshead of wine which was in his cellar to be pierced for them; and, with a hilarity which he delighted to indulge among his friends, desired

Steward [one of his friends] to send for some of it as long as it lasted, for he would not tarry until it was all drunk."[88]

As he came to the end, he asked his wife to read the fifteenth chapter of First Corinthians. "Is not that a comfortable chapter?" he said. Later that day, he said to his wife, "Go, read where I cast my first anchor." He was speaking of the text used when he had first trusted in Christ. She turned to the seventeenth chapter of John, and afterwards read to him from Calvin's sermons on the book of Ephesians. At eleven o'clock that night, Knox sighed deeply and said, "Now it is come." His servant Bannatyne drew near and urged him to think on the promises of Christ, which he used to preach to others, but Knox was now speechless, and so Bannatyne asked him to give a sign that he had heard, and that he was dying in peace. At this, John Knox raised up one of his hands, and then died without a struggle.[89]

Shortly before his death, things certainly looked grim for the Reformation. The St. Bartholomew's Day Massacre had been a devastating blow. All over France, tens of thousands of Huguenots were killed—butchered in unspeakable ways. Otto Scott observes an interesting turn in the demeanor of the great Reformer. "Knox was, in fact, dying. He knew it. He also knew that the strain of the protracted civil war had brought Scotland to its lowest point. In Europe a revitalized Vatican, armed with the great wealth and power of Spain, seemed destined for inevitable triumph . . . from all material signs, he had, or would, lose the cause for which he worked. Instead, he radiated calm. John Knox knew he had won."[90] This truly was an odd turn; during the course of his life Knox was the man who had correctly foreseen disaster tucked away in the recesses of great victories, but now he displayed the same gift, but looking in another direction. He now saw the triumph of the Reformation in the midst of significant setbacks. He died in peace, not only because he looked forward to heaven, but also because the work he had been given on earth was done—and he knew it could not be undone.

His funeral was on Wednesday, November 26th, and concluded with his burial in the churchyard at St. Giles. A throng of people, the aristocracy of the city, and the newly-elected Regent Morton attended the funeral. The eulogy was declared by Morton, often quoted because it was so self-evidently appropriate: "Here lies one who neither flattered nor feared any flesh."[91]

PART 2
THE CHARACTER OF JOHN KNOX

Can there be any greater blasphemy than to say,
God the Father has forgotten the benefits which he gave to
mankind in his only Son, Jesus?
—John Knox

The prelates and priests, whose horrible iniquity and insolent life
have infected all realms where they reign, have with their fathers,
the old Pharisees, taken away the key of knowledge.

—John Knox

LOVE

ACCORDING TO Scripture, the greatest achievements are worthless if love is not a present, animating, and driving force (1 Corinthians 13). Zeal alone for the things of God is not sufficient; a man must labor in the work of the kingdom in the manner in which the Lord of the kingdom requires. This is why the apostle Paul naturally links faith in God and love for His saints. "Therefore I also, after I heard of your faith in the Lord Jesus and your love for all the saints . . . (Ephesians 1:15)." According to this pattern, how does John Knox measure up? It is not enough that he was on "our side" in a great historical struggle, or that he accomplished some things that we have come to appreciate. Whenever we take the measure and weight of any man, we must be sure to use the canons and balances of heaven.

In speaking of prayer, Knox had nothing to do with a dry formalism. "Who will pray must know and understand that prayer is an earnest and familiar talking with God . . ."[1] This familiar discourse with the Father cannot be accomplished without the proper motivation. As he put it, "Such men verily declare themselves never to have understood what perfect prayer meant, nor to what end Jesus Christ commanded us to pray: which is, first, that our hearts may be inflammed with continual fear, honour, and love of God . . ."[2] In other words, the one who would pray properly must in the first place be *inflamed* with an ongoing fear, honor, and love of God. Modern Christians are not accustomed to couple such things as fear and love, but this simply shows that Knox understood the pattern of the New Testament in a way in which we do not. Peter, when speaking of the genuineness of faith, commends the believer to love the One he has not seen (1 Peter 1:8). At the same time we are instructed to work out our salvation with fear and *trembling* (Philippians 2:12). Not only did Knox love God, but did so with a biblical balance which is relatively rare in our day. In this, he serves as a godly example of an attitude that we need to recover.

Of course, our commitment to our fellow men tests our zeal for the honor of God. The first four of the Ten Commandments give us our duties to God, and the last six speak of our duties to men. This division of the law has traditionally been referred to as the first table and the second table of the law, respectively. The New Testament teaches us that our obedience to the second table is the stick by which we measure our dedication to the first. "If someone says, 'I love God,' and hates his brother, he is a liar; for he who does not love his brother whom he has seen, how can he love God whom he has not seen (1 John 4:20)?"

By all accounts, Knox was a loving and compassionate man in his personal dealings with others. This was one of the things that drove him in his ministry. He expressed true compassion toward those caught up in the vanity of false worship, but his central driving concern was for the "simple people" that had been deceived by the prevailing false doctrine. Many have taken his plain dealing in the pulpit as evidence that he was a cranky and sour man. However, this was not at all the case. In his circle of friends and acquaintances, he was well-loved, and he loved in return.

There is yet another test of love. It is one thing to say you love God, and we see that the point of testing is our treatment of our neighbor. To take this one step further, it is one thing to love a neighbor who treats you decently, and quite another to love those who have forfeited, at least from our earthly vantage point, any claims on our affection. Again, the Bible is clear. "For if you love those who love you, what reward have you? Do not even the tax collectors do the same (Matthew 5:46)?"

One of the most difficult times in Knox's life was the treatment he received from fellow Protestants in the debacle at Frankfurt. An open adversary is often easier to treat with Christian charity than a false friend and ally. Treachery is harder to forgive than honest opposition, and hypocrisy is often thought to justify hard feelings in return. Knox's opposition at Frankfurt had been stubborn and superstitious, and had attempted to place Knox in jeopardy through accusing him of treason. All this, not from the Roman Catholics, but from members of the same church! In Knox's account of the Frankfurt affair, he said, "O Lord God! Open their hearts to see their wickedness, and forgive them for thy manifold mercies. And I forgive them, O Lord, from the bottom of my heart."[3] Even this forgiveness may be looked upon as self-serving, as though Knox were acting the "spiritual" part. When Knox returned to Geneva, he wrote this as he prepared a written defense of his actions. However, on mature reflection, he decided not to publish it. Better to slander his own name, he thought, than to attack his Protestant brothers in their common cause. John Knox was a man who knew the meaning of biblical love.

REVERENCE

*T*HE FEAR of God was present throughout every single thing Knox did, but nowhere was it more evident than in his response to his call to the ministry. As subsequent events proved, John Knox did not suffer from stage fright. He was not reluctant to approach the ministry because it involved public speaking. He was a tutor, and did not at all mind speaking and teaching in informal settings.

However, preaching involves far more than what can be learned in seminary classes on homiletics. The apostle Paul considered the task of preaching this way: "For we are to God the fragrance of Christ among those who are being saved and among those who are perishing. To the one we are the aroma of death leading to death, and to the other the aroma of life leading to life. *And who is sufficient for these things?* For we are not, as so many, peddling the word of God; but as of sincerity, but as from God, we speak in the sight of God in Christ (2 Corinthians 2:15-17)." A man who preaches Christ is involved in eternal things, and his words provide the point of division between those who are saved and those who are lost. From the same sermon come the aroma of life and the stench of death. Who is sufficient for these things? Not the apostle Paul, and not John Knox.

When John Rough (a man of more slender attainments than Knox) preached a sermon on the authority that a congregation has to call ministers, he then turned to Knox and gave him his ministerial charge. "Overwhelmed by this unexpected and solemn charge, Knox, after an ineffectual attempt to address the audience, burst into tears, rushed out of the assembly, and shut himself up in his chamber."[4]

The prophet Jeremiah learned by bitter experience what it was to have the word of God shut up inside him, along with the responsibility to speak it. "Then I said, 'I will not make mention of Him, nor speak anymore in His name.' But His word was in my heart like a burning fire shut up in my bones; I was weary of holding it back, and I could not (Jeremiah 20:9)." Jeremiah knew that speaking the word of the Lord only got him into trouble. Nevertheless, at the same time, his office, and a deep understanding of the duties of that office, demanded that he speak.

By the time Knox was called to the ministry, he had a good understanding of the Scriptures, and of the doctrines of the Protestant faith. He also knew the political condition of Europe, and the persecuting zeal of the Roman church. Knox found himself holed up in a castle, surrounded by the Catholic power of the Scottish establishment, reinforced by the French. He knew what was coming, and knew that if he was called to the ministry of the Word, keeping silent was not an option. His ministry was therefore born in the fear of God, and, by the grace of God, it ended consistently in that same fear.

The laxity of the clergy in Scotland had not just been the path of least resistance, the way of all flesh—the corruption so far advanced that any kind of industry and zeal to fulfill the terms of the office was likely to bring suspicion of heresy, which in turn could bring death. It was therefore easy for anyone to hold the clerical laxity in contempt . . . as an observer. However, in the Protestant response, living according to a higher ministerial call involved more than just "hard work" and "laboring for souls." A man entering the ministry in those days, if he intended to keep his oath, had to reckon seriously with the possibility that he would soon find himself tied to a stake with flames at his feet. So on the natural level, the ministry was no place for the effeminate, and on the spiritual level, a reverent man like John Knox found himself confronted with insuperable difficulties. The early Protestant preachers did not think their message was to get the sick patients to take their medicine. They saw their task as one of preaching in a graveyard, praying for a resurrection. "Son of man can these bones live?" Oh, sovereign Lord, you know.

Knox did not just have a doctrine that the ministry was a high calling. He also held that a sovereign God had the right to call ill-equipped men to that office, and that if He did so, the ill-equipped men were in no position to talk back. To the end of his life, he believed himself to be ill-equipped. Further, his premonitions of hazard all came true, and on more than one occasion he had to preach a sermon in the lion's mouth. John Knox struggled with temptation and sin, as we all do, but we do not have any historical evidence that he ever backed away from something he believed to be the truth of God because he feared the response of man. We must understand this, not as a personality feature of Knox (brashness, say), but rather as a gracious gift of God. What God gave to him was the gift of reverence. "He sent redemption unto his people: he hath commanded his covenant for ever: holy and reverend is *his* name (Psalm 111:9, AV)."

Courage

*J*OHN KNOX fled from Bloody Mary in 1553. Once on the Continent, he wrote letters of fierce exhortation to his brethren left behind. C.S. Lewis remarks, "It is impossible to suppress the uneasy remembrance (even though we dare make no judgement) that these fiery exhortations are uttered by a man in safety to men in horrible danger."[5]

It is good that Lewis made no settled judgment here, despite the hint of a judgment, and the obvious and notable problem. Exhortations to courage made by those away from the action rarely come across well.[6] Knox himself was well aware of these appearances, and noted in a letter that he had not fled because he was primarily concerned about his own physical safety. In a letter to Mrs. Bowes, he says, "But my fleeing is no matter; by God's grace I may come to battle before that all the conflict be ended."[7]

In ancient times, the great Trojan hero Hector was flawed in a way that Knox was not. He was afraid of . . .

being thought afraid. Because of this, he felt led to attempt things that his better judgment should have discouraged. Knox was not in this category at all. He wanted nothing more than to be in the battle, in the front lines, when the time and circumstances were right. In a very real way, he was built for battle and he looked forward eagerly to the right time and place. While he no doubt began with a very natural physical courage, he had also been shown the grace of God and had learned to fear God. The first thing a right fear of God drives away is a fear of man.

Thomas Cranmer, an archbishop of Canterbury during this time, provides us with a good example of a reformer whose courage failed him at one point, and who then returned to his first love and died with great courage. For fear of his life, he had recanted his Protestant convictions. Later he repented, and boldly declared his faith just before he was immediately hustled out to the stake, and there burned. When fire was put to the wood:

> Cranmer achieved a final serenity; and he fulfilled the promise which he had made in his last shouts in the church: "forasmuch as my hand offended, writing contrary to my heart, my hand shall first be punished there-for." He stretched it out into the heart of the fire, for all the spectators to see. [8]

Knox's flight from Mary was not in this category, and his subsequent (and indubitable) courage was not a sign of "repentance." He sought to serve Christ by fleeing, and he looked forward to the time when he could serve Christ in the front of the battle. Cranmer was more naturally timid than Knox, while others had to persuade Knox to flee. Christ had told his followers that flight from persecution was an honorable option (Matthew 10:23), but also, just a few verses later, that denial of His name was always dishonorable (Matthew 10:33). John Knox certainly knew that strategic withdrawal is sometimes an important part of kingdom work. However, when the battle was joined, and the issues were defined and clear, no one was more stalwart than John Knox. "And albeit I have, in the beginning of this battle, appeared to play the faint-hearted and feeble soldier (the cause of which I remit to God), yet my prayer is that I may be restored to the battle again."[9] Knox knew the appearance, and he knew the reality.

Apart from this flight from Mary Tudor, Knox had many other opportunities to demonstrate his complete fearlessness. When summoned to appear before a persecuting council, he did so, and caused the council to disband in consternation. He was willing to rebuke royalty whether or not powerful friends surrounded him. He was willing to defy idolatry while a galley slave, and this while in the hands of those who could have treated him very harshly. Nothing exhibited his courage more than his determination to preach at St. Andrews after receiving a threat from the bishop there. The bishop had said that he planned to welcome Knox with a twelve-gun salute, the greater part of which "would light upon his nose."[10] Knox showed up nonetheless, and preached without the bishop fulfilling the threat.

It is fair to say that Knox was feared by his opponents; it would be quite inaccurate to say that he feared them. Many attended the funeral of Knox, including the newly-elected regent, Morton. This man, a very practical politician, gave a most fitting eulogy to the character of John Knox. "There," he said, "lies he who never feared the face of man."[11]

MERCY

$\mathcal{F}$ROM OUR vantage, Knox's demeanor certainly seems austere and stern to many, but McCrie points out a common mistake made by superficial students of history. "Those who have charged him with insensibility and inhumanity, have fallen into a mistake very common with superficial thinkers, who, in judging of the character of persons who lived in a state of society very different from their own, have pronounced upon their moral qualities from the mere aspect of their exterior manners."[12] Manners, like clothing, change from age to age, but God's standard of morality does not. Our photographs from an earlier era hardly show anyone smiling, and today everyone smiles for the camera. To judge from this that our era is the more cheerful of the two would be a great mistake indeed. This is our custom, not our heart.

Knox certainly does confront brutal cruelty with brutal courage, and language to match. "O cruel serpent! In vain do you spend your venom. For the days of God's elect you cannot shorten! And when the wheat corn is fallen on the ground, then does it most multiply."[13] The strength of this kind of polemic, which some in our day might think inconsistent with a spirit of mercy, was certainly not inconsistent in his age.

John Knox knew himself to be a representative of God. "And therefore take heed betimes; God calls upon you; beware that you shut not up your ears. Judge not the matter after the vility [lowliness] of my body, whom God has appointed ambassador and messenger unto you; but with reverence and fear consider him whose message I bear."[14] However, this representation most certainly had to include the characteristics of God's mercy, not just His judgments. This is why, alongside Knox's thunderings, we find that a full understanding of mercy tempered his moral courage.

> He was austere, not unfeeling; stern, not savage; vehement, not vindictive. There is not an instance of his employing his influence to revenge any personal injury which he had received. Rigid as his maxims respecting the execution of justice were, there are numerous instances on record of his interceding for the pardon of criminals; and, unless when crimes were atrocious, or when the welfare of the state was in the most imminent danger, he never exhorted the executive government to the exercise of severity.[15]

A lot has been written, or assumed, about the severity, bloodiness, and intolerance of Knox and his Presbyterians. Here we come to a true historical curiosity. Certain periods in history, and the positions represented by them, have a reputation for urbanity, broadness, civility, and tolerance. The Elizabethan era, for example, gave us Shakespeare, and was a time that entirely suppressed those supposedly "intolerant" Puritans. But during that time, with the full concurrence of the Anglican bishops, at least 124 Catholic priests were put to death in England for conscience' sake, along with as many as fifty-seven laymen and women. And during the same time period in Scotland, home of the intolerant, we find that *two* were judicially put to death for their religion, and those two were probably a confused reporting of just one incident.[16] When we consider the historical record, we find that the most "intolerant" by reputation have often actually proven to have been the most merciful.

This pattern of selective reporting has occurred over and over again in the history of the Reformation and its heirs—Calvin repeatedly sought to spare Servetus by seeking to persuade him not to come to Geneva. At the Salem witch trials, we find that pressure from the Puritan ministers of New England actually *suppressed* them. When the Protestant faith was established in Scotland, the result was not what many assume—persecutorial zeal was not in evidence. We saw earlier that the man who had been spared from execution—through the intercession of Knox—had assassinated the good regent, Moray.

This is not to say that the early Protestants repudiated the power of the sword. In Scotland, men like Gillespie and Rutherford wrote in defense of the authority the magistrate had to defend true religion, but this view was *not* distinctively Protestant. "All parties inherited from the Middle Ages the assumption that Christian man could live only in a theocratic polity which had both the right and the duty of enforcing true religion by persecution. Those who resisted its authority did so not because they thought it had no right to impose doctrines but because they thought it was imposing the wrong ones."[17] What *was* distinctively Protestant was the reluctance they exhibited to use the power they believed themselves to possess. This reluctance was borne of mercy, and was exhibited in great measure in John Knox—severity where necessary, and mercy whenever possible.

Another last qualification is necessary. The Protestants were not averse to shedding blood. As Boettner comments, "However the fact is to be explained it is true that the Calvinists were the only fighting Protestants."[18] However, it has to be said that for the most part they did so honestly, openly, on the field of battle. Their faith was a compound mixture of all that the Bible teaches, and this results in some combinations that are strange to us. They were both warriors and martyrs, both warlike . . . and merciful.

BALANCE

SOMEONE IN the business world once said that a reasonable man never accomplished anything. This seems to us to have some wisdom about it. Surely great accomplishment requires extreme dedication, and extreme dedication must at least border on the monomaniacal. This, we think, is not likely to result in balanced individuals. Olympic figure skaters have to start training when they are four years old, and perhaps we all remember that kid who expressed his desire to be president during the student council elections in eighth grade.

However, despite his fierce dedication to the reform of the Church, we must describe John Knox as a *balanced* individual. First, he was theologically balanced. Although a firm believer in predestination, he did not fall into the errors of those who get hold of only one end of a truth, and who then wave it around until they hurt themselves. "This I write, because some men are so severe, that they would not that we should ask bodily health of God, because the sickness is sent to us by him. But such men do not rightly understand . . ."[19] Some in Knox's day thought that because God was sovereign, then it followed that we should sit back and "take it," whatever "it" might be. Whatever God decided to dish out, it was our duty to receive without complaint and without trying to avoid the blow in any way, but Knox knew his Bible better than this. The God who told us that all things come from His hand also told us that we are to employ means to obtain those things. For example, we are to ask God for our daily bread (Matthew 6:11), and thank Him for it when it comes (1 Corinthians 11:24). At the same time, we are told in no uncertain terms that we are to work for our food (2 Thessalonians 3:10). The doctrine of predestination was a much-roiled topic during the Reformation, and Knox himself wrote a very learned treatise on the subject. During times of theological controversy, it is easy to go to theological extremes, which Knox did not do at all.[20]

Knox also displayed what we might call a firm political balance. He did not adopt the common expedient of justifying whatever is done by our side in the name of our side. Recall that John Knox was called to the ministry in the midst of a hostage situation, a situation inaugurated by the assassination of the cardinal. As soon as he was called to this ministry, he began to reprove sin—and not the sin of those outside the castle, but rather of those inside it. He did not preach against the wickedness that forced them to hide in the castle; he preached against the wickedness that was likely to overthrow the cause of those taking refuge in the castle. "From the time that he was chosen to be their preacher, he had openly rebuked these disorders; and when he perceived that his admonitions failed in putting a stop to them, he did not conceal his apprehensions of the unsuccessful issue of the enterprise in which they were engaged."[21]

In other words, Knox was not a blind partisan. He had settled convictions, but those convictions were based upon what the Bible taught, and not upon the battle lines drawn up by self-professed Protestants. When Protestants were guilty of wickedness, Knox would identify it as such. He did this because he feared God, and lived before Him. He knew that the Reformation could not succeed if those involved in the work of it in any way angered God. This meant that he could not be "pragmatic" or "realistic" about sin in the camp. The Israelites had been defeated in their assault on Ai because of the hidden sin of Achan (Joshua 7:20). How much more, then, should the Protestants be careful about the toleration of *open* sin in their own ranks?

Knox displayed his character trait of balance again during the Frankfurt affair, when "our Reformer displayed the greatest moderation and forbearance, while the conduct of his opponents was marked throughout with violence and want of charity."[22] An unbalanced individual does not understand which situations call for compromise, and which call for taking a stand on a central principle. An unbalanced individual drives his car at one speed, whether he is on the freeway or driving through a sleepy neighborhood. However, Knox was not like this; he had a firm grasp of what issues were of first importance, and on which there could be no compromise. He also knew which were the issues where *he* could not bend, but where his Christian brothers might differ. He knew where the law of Christ required him to set aside what he believed to be the most proper (and biblical) course—for the sake of a broader unity. At Frankfurt, Knox was willing to use a liturgy that he believed was deficient, because God required it. Unfortunately, his adversaries there did not have the same temper of mind.

Ironically, those who cannot see Knox making all these adjustments are themselves displaying the kind of imbalance of which they accuse him. It is not that Knox was heinous enough to commit any sin, but rather that, for some of his accusers, any stick at all is good enough to beat him with.

TENDERNESS

*J*OHN KNOX was a tender man. In the midst of one of his blunt confrontations of Mary Queen of Scots he responded to the queen in a very gentle way. The collision was over Knox's opposition to the possibility of the queen marrying a papist—a marriage that Knox knew would threaten the Reformation. As a result of a sermon in which he had expressed this opposition, the queen summoned Knox to appear before her—his fourth visit with Mary.

Asked about his position, Knox replied, "Whensoever the nobility of this realm shall consent that ye be subject to an unfaithful husband, they do as much as in them lieth to renounce Christ, to banish his truth from them, to betray the freedom of this realm, and perchance shall in the end do small comfort to yourself."[23] Knox was simply unwilling to jeopardize the cause of Christ through a convenient marriage for the queen. For the modern reader, I should state that marriages of royalty in those days were public policy issues, affairs of state. In other words, Knox was not intruding himself into a private matter.

At these words, the queen burst into tears, with great sobbing and weeping. Knox stood quietly until she was done, and then protested that he never took pleasure in the distress of anyone, and that it was with great difficulty that he could stand to see his own boys weep when he had to discipline them. Still less could he delight in her majesty's tears, but his conscience was constrained. He could not stand by in silence and be quiet when the commonwealth was threatened. In short, even in the midst of a great dis-agreement, he demonstrated tenderness to his adversary the queen. The fact that the queen did not appreciate it (which she most certainly did not) does not mean that Knox was harsh or unkind.

This tenderness was in evidence during his time as a galley slave also:

> The prisoners in Mont St. Michel consulted Knox, as to the lawfulness of attempting to escape by breaking their prison, which was opposed by some of them, lest their escape should subject their brethren who remained in confinement to more severe treatment. He returned for answer, that such fears were not a sufficient reason for relinquishing the design, and that they might, with a safe conscience, effect their escape, provided it could be done "without the blood of any shed or spilt; but to shed any man's blood for their freedom, he would never consent."[24]

Knox was unwilling to prevent the freedom of others because of the trouble it might cause those left behind, including himself. Neither was he willing to allow the escaping prisoners to shed the blood of any of their captors.

He was equipped to be a tender pastor. His own mother-in-law, Mrs. Bowes, suffered for many years from plaguing religious doubts, and Knox was able to speak to her condition with a gentleness borne of long practice. In an exposition of the sixth Psalm, addressed to her, he wrote, "I remember that often you have complained upon the grudging and murmuring that you found within yourself, fearing that it provoked God to more displeasure. Behold and consider, dear mother, what God has borne with his saints before. Will he not bear the same with you, being most sorry for your imperfection? He cannot do otherwise."[25] A little later, he again encourages her as his beloved mother—"Yet if the heart can only sob unto God, despair not; you shall obtain your heart's desire, and you are not destitute of faith."[26]

The saints who were persecuted for their faith also filled Knox with tenderness. He spoke feelingly about "the tears of widows oppressed, of orphans left comfortless, of prisoners wrongfully tormented, and of the banished (who sustain hunger and other calamities in strange countries),"[27] all because they would not renounce their faith in Christ.

Speaking of Knox's style of writing, C.S. Lewis commented, "It might be supposed that to read a body of work so occasional, so little varied in subject-matter, and so fierce in temper, was a hard task. In reality, the surprising thing is that it is not harder. He has humour; in places he even has tenderness. But his chief merit is his style."[28] Lewis has many of the common prejudices about Knox, but being a fair-minded critic and reader, he is able to see what most others do not see—a tender-hearted Christian. His surprise is still evident—"he *even* has tenderness;" but those who share Knox's general theology and worldview are not so surprised. Given the teaching of the Scriptures as a whole, we should expect ferocity and tenderness to lie down, side by side, like the lion and lamb.[29]

Humility

*I*N MANY circles, pride and leadership seem to go together. Christ knew this would be a temptation in His Church, and so plainly warned His disciples about it. "And He sat down, called the twelve, and said to them, 'If anyone desires to be first, he shall be last of all and servant of all (Mark 9:35).'" Natural boldness and zeal is not enough for leadership in the kingdom of God. A man must be meek before God before he can stand upright before lawless thrones. How can an arrogant prophet rebuke an arrogant king? Moses was the meekest man on the face of the earth, the Bible tells us, and yet he was the one able to withstand Pharaoh. Meekness before God is not weakness before men. In fact, such meekness and humility before God is essential if any man is to be truly used by God.

John Knox had no delusions about himself in the light of God's perfection. He knew that the infinite clarity of God's gaze had to see completely what he himself knew only partially. During the reign of Edward, Knox recalled that he had in truth preached the true gospel. "But alas! I did it not with such fervency, with such indifferency, and with such diligence, as this day I know my duty was to have done."[30] He is confessing here a sin of omission; he could have done more. During the reign of Edward, the time proving to be so short—he should have done more. "But, alas! This day my conscience accuses me, that I spoke not so plainly as my duty was to have done."[31] It is the same kind of confession here; he spoke plainly, but not *so* plainly as he should have.

Many moderns do not understand how the early Protestants could feel such a great sense of religious relief and at the same time be pretty severe with themselves. The answer lay in the doctrine of justification. They knew God received them based upon the merit and virtue of Christ's perfect righteousness only. "We want, above all, to know what it felt like to be an early Protestant . . . All the initiative has been on God's side; all has been free unbounded grace. And all will continue to be free, unbounded grace. His own puny and ridiculous efforts would be as helpless to retain the joy as they would have been to achieve it in the first place."[32] Utterly forgiven, and all by God's grace in Christ, the early Protestants could scrutinize their failings and sins. All this done in much the same way that a boy might study an ugly tooth that had caused him so much pain . . . after it was out. "I openly confess the fruit and virtue of Christ's body, of his blood and passion, to appertain to myself; and that I am a member of his mystical body; and that God the Father is appeased with me, notwithstanding my first corruption and present infirmities."[33] Knox knew that the Father was not angry with him, for Christ's sake, and he knew his present corruption. That corruption was a grief to him, but not a *threat* to him.

Knox also knew the dangers and temptations of "worm theology," the practice of making oneself out to be a very despicable sinner, because that is the way we brag around here. False humility is itself a form of pride. "Think not, beloved of the Lord, that I thus accuse myself without just cause, as though in so doing I might appear more holy . . . I know myself grievously to have offended the majesty of my God, during the time that Christ's gospel had free passage in England."[34] In some circles, the way to appear most holy is to lament how *unholy* you are, but Knox was aware of all such head games; he really believed that he was objectively guilty of being less zealous than he should have been during the reign of Edward. And, being guilty, he should not hide it, or seek to cover it up.

He was also aware of his sin of an ungodly partiality. "For, in preaching Christ's gospel, albeit mine eye (as God knows) was not much upon worldly promotion, yet the love of friends, and carnal affection of some men with whom I was most familiar, allured me to make more residence in one place than in another, having more respect to the pleasure of a few, than to the necessity of many."[35] Knox confesses these sins, not because he wants to call attention to himself, but rather because he knows that Edward was removed because of God's displeasure with His people. The duty of the people is therefore to repent of their sins, and their leaders and pastors must show them how.

John Knox had a good understanding of how personal humility equips a man to serve the people of God. In a discussion of the apostle Peter's failures, Knox taught that God had a purpose in this as well. " . . . as though Christ should have said, 'Peter, you are yet too proud to be a pastor. You cannot stoop, nor bow your back down to take up the weak sheep. You do not yet know your own infirmity and weakness, and therefore you can do nothing but despise the weak ones.'"[36]

A pastor has to know his own infirmities, and confess them in humility. If he does not, then he will be severe with the lambs and sheep of Christ's fold, and this, as Knox well knew, was a pastoral monstrosity.

ADVERSARIES

*G*REAT MEN have great enemies, and in this John Knox was no exception. Greatness is usually not the result of talents and abilities standing alone, but rather the result of a confrontation between a man of ability and a time of great moment. An important part of the conditions for such a time of "great moment" includes opposition by people of comparable ability or power.

John Knox had great and powerful enemies, and he opposed them honestly. McCrie quotes one historian, a man who was no Reformed partisan, who said that Knox "immortalized himself by his courage against Popery, and his firmness against the tyranny of Mary; and that though a violent, he was always an open and honourable, enemy to the Catholics."[37] The Bible never tells us to have no enemies, but it does say how we are to conduct our warfare.

His first great enemy was the Roman Catholic church. G.K. Chesterton, himself a Catholic, once commented that a brave man should be willing to attack anything he believes to be an error, no matter how formidable, but, he went on to say, there *are* some errors too big to patronize. Too many modern Protestants belong to churches that were planted in 1978, and despite this, they have the audacity to dismiss the Catholic Church as "a sect." That case can and should be made, but not by people who think of 1776 as ancient history.

Knox was not in this category at all. He took the power of the Roman church seriously, as well as their arguments. He was willing, if given a Bible and the liberty of his tongue, to meet with them in any venue in order to contrast the teaching of Scripture with what they represented it to be. In the ongoing battle with the Roman church, the reformers knew that they were battling powers that had been entrenched for centuries. These powers had departed from the ancient paths, but they had not done this the day before yesterday. In calling them back to the pattern of the primitive church, Knox well knew his position in history and the authority mounted against him. Like David against Goliath, we measure him by the size of his enemy.

His second great enemy was Mary Queen of Scots. She was a woman of considerable intelligence, charm, cunning, beauty, and ruthlessness. She had been brought up in the court of France, one of the world's great powers, and she was unaccustomed to opposition, least of all opposition from a commoner like Knox. Though she was unaccustomed to such challenges, she still met them. This was a conflict between beauty and the beast, but the predictably fulfilled roles were not. The heart of the beauty was cold and murderous, and the rough exterior of the beast encased one of the most tender hearts in Scotland. Be that as it may, the collisions between Mary and Knox are legendary, and while Mary was not a worthy woman, she was still a significant adversary. In many ways, the character of Knox would have been unrevealed without her.

It is in some ways difficult to select such representatives, because Knox had so many good enemies. His third enemy of note was within the Protestant camp —Secretary Maitland. Although a man of considerable learning and ability, Maitland is more important to us here as a representative of a class of people, which is to say, temporizing Protestants. Whenever a great change is brought about by men of vision, who do not love the sounds of compromise, the fruits of that victory are commonly parceled out by men who come bustling up ten minutes after the battle (a battle they solemnly warned against), all eager now to share in the spoil. First thing you know, the place is crawling with suits and haircuts, administrators and PR men, management consultants and bean counters. This is not a modern phenomenon. In the Scottish reformation, one of the great stumbling blocks was the standing wealth and income of the Roman church in Scotland. Among other things, this resulted in the sorry spectacle of Protestants ordaining "tulchan bishops." A tulchan was a calfskin filled with straw, placed as an inducement to make a cow give up her milk more freely. This modified episcopacy was a joke, and a moral disgrace. However, temporizing has its rewards, and Knox was a consistent opponent of all such compromising with self-interest. As discussed elsewhere, he was more than willing to compromise *where principle demanded it,* but he was constant against men on his own side whose counsels called for expediency.

Knox clearly displayed this in the debate that occurred between him and Maitland over the opposition shown to Mary Queen of Scots by the Protestant ministers. A nominal Protestant, Maitland was in the queen's cabinet, and the zeal of the Protestant courtiers was growing cold. The ministers preached and prayed accordingly, and a clash was inevitable. At the resultant debate, Maitland's presentation was "embellished with learning, but prone to subtlety" and Knox displayed a "vigorous understanding," one "delighting in bold sentiments, and superior to all fear."[38] Maitland was a type similar to those we have in every age who urge realistic and pragmatic counsels, and Knox was a type of man who cares more for faithfulness than success—and finds that success comes to him.

This is not said to honor the enemies of Knox in such a way as to indicate that Knox should not have considered them enemies. At the same time, we must acknowledge that in stature, they were worthy of him.

Study

$\mathcal{W}$E CANNOT really understand the Reformation unless we see it as a recovery of a certain kind of scholarship and learning. However, it was not merely academic; because it was the work of the Spirit of God, the Reformation was scholarship on fire. In many respects it was an essential part of the Renaissance, whatever that was. C.S. Lewis comments on the difficulty of using the word with any degree of precision. "Where we have a noun we tend to imagine a thing. The word *Renaissance* helps to impose a factitious unity on all the untidy and heterogeneous events which were going on in those centuries as in any others."[39]

To say that the Reformation and Renaissance involved a recovery of learning would be wildly inaccurate—medieval man was a great lover of books. Rather, it would be more helpful to say that a new attitude toward learning had developed, and this new attitude created a tremendous thirst for expanding knowledge. It was a time of exploration—the Americas discovered, and the world opened up. The printing press had also been invented, and so ancient worlds also opened up—ancient writers, church fathers, and pagan philosophers. The cry in the Reformation was *ad fontes,* back to the sources. A great part of this new world was a rediscovery of old worlds. This all required scholarship more broad and aggressive than had been common in the medieval period.

In Scotland particularly, the established authorities regarded the new scholarship as dangerous. The learning of the old scholasticism could run deep, but it also tended to run in narrow and predictable channels. Striking out in new directions was not encouraged. The martyr George Wishart had first come under suspicion because he was teaching Greek, and so "learning was branded as the parent of heresy."[40]

This is why, in one of his first controversies, John Knox was galled to have to admit his ignorance of Hebrew. "In the Hebrew tongue I confess myself ignorant, but have (as God knows) fervent thirst to have some entrance therein: and so of the Hebrew diction cannot contend."[41] Here was a man who wanted to have as many weapons as he could obtain. Not having access to the Old Testament in the original was a real problem to Knox, and in this regard, his time on the Continent was time well spent.

> *Knox returned to Geneva, and applied himself to study with all the ardour of youth, although his age now bordered upon fifty* [actually closer to thirty-five, ed.]. *It seems to have been at this time that he made himself master of the Hebrew language, which he had no opportunity of acquiring in early life.* [42]

He was not what we would call a religious enthusiast, one working on the emotions and prejudices of crowds. God calls us to love Him with all our brains, and Knox knew and appreciated the value of hard study. During his time in Geneva, he pastored a small congregation of English exiles. Despite the size of the congregation (around 200 people), it contained some highly educated men. Among the seniors (what we would call elders) were men like Miles Coverdale, a translator of the Bible, John Bodley and his son Thomas, the founder of the Bodleian Library, Thomas Bentley, a distinguished expert in Hebrew, and later bishop at Lichfield, and James Pilkington, who became bishop of Durham. The congregation also included John Foxe, famous for his *Book of Martyrs.* In addition, the congregation included about ten students studying for the ministry.[43] It is not at all surprising that this group could really produce. "During that year [1558] he was engaged, along with several learned men of his congregation, in making a new translation of the Bible into English; which, from the place where it was composed and first printed, has obtained the name of the Geneva Bible."[44] This Bible, along with others, provided a strong, albeit unacknowledged, basis for much of the King James Version of the Bible.

The popular caricature of Knox is that of a rabble-rouser, found in a tavern somewhere, given a few Calvinistic ideas, and sent off to make some trouble for the authorities. Actually, he studied at St. Andrews University under one of the finest scholastics of Europe, John Major. He was a friend and confidant of some of the greatest minds of Europe, which at that time were overwhelmingly Reformed and Protestant. Chief among them was John Calvin, who knew and respected Knox's intellectual abilities.

This is hard for us to comprehend, in part because of how scholarship today tends to eviscerate those who involve themselves in it, but Knox, although a great scholar, was more interested in truth than in research grants, more zealous for righteousness than for a general collegiality. He had a great mind and was highly educated, but he was not what *we* would describe as an intellectual.

Humor

*A*S MIGHT be expected, the humor of Knox is dry and very . . . Scottish. He, like many of his countrymen, was a master of humorous and ironic understatement. In his private life, among friends and acquaintances, he was accustomed to unwind a little. " . . . he relished the pleasures of society, and, among his acquaintances, was accustomed to unbend his mind, by indulging in innocent recreation, and in the sallies of wit and humour to which he had a strong propensity, notwithstanding the graveness of his general deportment."[45] Those close to him were privileged to enjoy his very developed sense of humor. He was this way throughout his life, and, as mentioned earlier, even when death was approaching, he was able to sit with some of his friends and engage in a great deal of hilarity, *which was his custom.*[46]

Few things are more terrible in human society than the humorless reformer, and it was fortunate indeed that Knox was not in that number. The humorless reformer is a man who cannot see what he most needs to see, which is his own contribution to the problem. In this vain and fallen world, a man who cannot laugh has no business undertaking to cure the world's ills, because he is chief among them.[47] John Knox was wiser than to think that the Church could be reformed apart from laughter.

His humor was not limited to private conversation among friends, however, and even in the great battles over truth, he does not lose his sense of humor. Of course, the humor there can be somewhat grim, suitable to the occasion. While describing Knox's history of the Reformation in Scotland, C.S. Lewis says, "Knox's humour, as becomes a countryman of Dunbar, is more boisterous and ferocious."[48] Sometimes moderns might not even recognize the humor at all. Although the fight was deadly serious, Knox had a ready eye for incongruities. In one place, Knox records the threat made against him by the bishop of St. Andrews—the threat mentioned earlier which was in itself pretty funny. Knox would be received, the bishop's man said, with a twelve-gun salute, the most part of which "should light upon his nose." Knox quotes this with obvious appreciation, and his marginalia records his comment on it. "The Bishop's good mind toward John Knox."[49]

At other places, his humor approaches that of a high farce. In one incident recounted by Knox, some Protestants had waylaid a procession in honor of St. Giles, the patron saint of Scotland. In the scuffling that followed, the image of the saint toppled over, and one of the Protestants occupied himself with "dadding his head to the calsay," which is to say, "beating the image's head on the road." A sober scholar or uptight historian, as some view Knox, did not write the description of what followed this affair.

*There might have been seen so sudden a fray as seldom
has been seen amongst that sort of men within this
realm; for down goes the crosses, off goes the surplice,
round caps corner with the crowns. The Grey Friars
gaped, the Black Friars blew, the priests panted and
fled; and happy was he that first got the house; for
such a sudden fray came never amongst the generation
of Antichrist within this realm before.* [50]

In another earlier incident, Knox was happy to
describe a collision between rivals within the Catholic
church. Cardinal Beaton and the archbishop of Glasgow
had quite a rivalry going between themselves, and one
time when they were in the same town, a competition
arose as to whose cross should be borne in preeminence,
obviously an important question. "Coming forth (or going
in, all is one) at the choir door of Glasgow Kirk, begins
striving for state betwix the two cross-bearers, so that from
glowming [scowling] they come to shouldering; from
shouldering, they go to buffets, and from dry blows, by
neffs and neffeling [fisticuffs] . . ." [51] All this, no doubt, was
quite in keeping with Christ's observation that the first
would be last, and the last first (Matthew 19:30).

The end result was not pretty. "And then began no little
fray, but yet a merry game; for rochets were rent, tippets
were torn, crowns were knapped [cracked], and side gowns
might have been seen wantonly wag from the one wall to
the other. Many of them lacked beards, and that was the
more pity; and therefore could not bukkill other by the birse
[grapple with each other by the beard], as bold men would
have done." [52] A question as to whose cross should have
the greater honor? As Knox put it succinctly in the
margin—"A question worthy of such two prelates." [53]

OBEDIENCE

*I*T IS easy to have strong views on the subject of authority, but these usually come up when we are considering how someone else ought to be obeying us. When we turn to consider those that *we* should be obeying, our ardor sometimes dims. Consequently, a good way of measuring a man's true view of authority is therefore to examine how well he defers to and submits to others. It is not wise to entrust a man with authority who does not know himself how to submit to authority. Any man in leadership who demands submission or obedience should be prepared for the request, "Show us how."

Of course, all obedience is due in the first place to the Word of God. In a letter to the Queen-regent Mary of Guise, Knox taught her that such obedience to God was the foundation of all true civil authority.

> *Lay the book of God before your eyes, and let it be*
> *judge to that which I say; which if you with fear and*

> *reverence obey, as did Josiah the admonitions of the*
> *prophetess, then shall he (by whom kings reign) crown*
> *your battle with double benediction, and reward you*
> *with wisdom, riches, glory, honour, and long life in this*
> *your temporal regiment, and with everlasting life, when*
> *the King of all kings . . . the Lord Jesus, shall appear to*
> *judgment . . .*[54]

In other words, she should not ground her rule of Scotland on commanding, but rather on submitting. This submission rendered not to Knox, or to any other man, but rather to the God of heaven alone. Uninstructed by the Word, we tend to think that the way to advance is clamber up, but the Bible teaches that the way up is down, and the last shall be first.

Knox claimed that the Word alone was his final and ultimate authority, and this demeanor of scriptural submission, when it is genuine, tends to show up in other relationships as well. Headstrong or unwilling to listen to others is in no way a fitting description for Knox. For example, Knox believed that Geneva was "the most perfect school of Christ that ever was in the earth since the days of the apostles. In other places I confess Christ to be truly preached; but manners and religion to be so sincerely reformed, I have not yet seen in any other place beside."[55] Having come to this conclusion, when Knox came to Geneva, he came prepared to study and learn. He had a respected place among the leaders of the Reformation, but this was not because he pushed himself forward—quite the reverse.

When a call came from the English congregation at Frankfurt, he received the advice of those in Geneva to go. He was not individualistic in his decision-making. Later when he received the call to return to Scotland, he did the same. "Knox, at the same time that he laid this letter before his congregation, craved the advice of Calvin and the other ministers of Geneva. They gave it as their opinion. 'that he could not refuse the call without showing himself rebellious to God, and unmerciful to his country.'"[56] In the multitude of counselors there is wisdom, and Knox is one who sought advice from many godly and wise men.

He did not just do this when it came to "administrative issues." He was "instructable" on doctrinal issues as well. After he fled from England, he sought instruction from the Protestant leaders there on a doctrine of civil resistance that he was in the process of developing. In this doctrine, he did advance somewhat beyond many of the Protestant doctors, but he did not do it in isolation—he sought out their counsel and correction. It was a very practical question, and one on which Knox had to himself give advice to the Protestant lords back in Scotland. In one letter to them, "he also communicates his advice on the delicate question of resistance to supreme rulers. They [the Scottish lords] had consulted him on this subject, and he had submitted it to the judgment of the most learned men on the Continent."[57]

In 1 Timothy 3:2, Paul mentions that a Christian bishop must be "apt to teach." It is of course true that teachers should be able to teach, and the Bible gives us this same requirement elsewhere, but here there is at least the possibility that the word should be translated *teachable*. Men who aspire to leadership in the Church are frequently those who are quick with words and able to speak in public. Less common is the demeanor of humble and ready acceptance of wisdom from others. If this is in fact the teaching of the passage, John Knox found himself blessed with such a teachable spirit. He did not allow himself to be instructed by the ignorant and heretical, but he did confess himself as needing the accountability provided by other minds.

An obedient man, he looked for more accountability than simply hearing the sound of his own voice.

CHURCHMAN

*J*OHN KNOX was a dedicated churchman, in no way given to factionalism or a sectarian spirit. Knox demonstrates this in many ways. Many modern readers of history fail to see the *catholicity* of the Reformation. In no way did the reformers desire to found "a denomination" in the modern sense; rather, they desired the reformation of the one Church. They were one party within the Church; the other party was the papal faction.

In a letter given to their parliament, the Scottish Protestants saw the struggle as one occurring *within* the Church. Knox probably wrote the letter. It said, in part, "Seeing that the controversy in religion, which long hath continued betwix the Protestants of Almany [Germany], Helvetia [Switzerland], and other provinces, and the Papistical Church, is not yet decided by a lawful and General Council; and seeing that our consciences are likewise touched with the fear of God, as was theirs in the beginning of their controversy, we most humbly desire, that all such Acts of Parliament, as in the time of darkness gave power to the Church men to execute their tyranny against us, by reason that we to them were delated as heretics, may be suspended and abrogated, till a General Council lawfully assembled have decided all controversies in religion."[58] Far from desiring schism, the first Protestants looked to a General Council, which could settle the reform of the Church.

When it came to the reform of the polity of the Church, Knox had set opinions, but even in this instance, he was not a sectarian perfectionist. "As early as the year 1547, he [had] taught, in his first sermons at St. Andrews, that no mortal man could be head of the Church."[59] And yet, after this, he was willing to labor as a chaplain to King Edward (the mortal head of the Church of England) toward the eventual full reformation of the Church. The king so appreciated his labors within the Anglican communion that he offered Knox the office of bishop. "Edward VI, with the concurrence of his privy council, offered him a bishopric. But he rejected it; and in the reasons which he gave for his refusal, declared the episcopal office to be destitute of divine authority in itself, and its exercise in the English Church to be inconsistent with the ecclesiastical canons. This is attested by Beza, a contemporary author."[60]

However, his theological rejection of the legitimacy of this office was not the only reason for turning it down. "What moved me to refuse, and that with displeasure of all men (even of those who best loved me), those high promotions which were offered by him, whom God has taken from us for our offences? Assuredly the foresight of trouble to come."[61] Knox foresaw the troubles of the times of Bloody Mary and knew that the obligations of the office of bishop would complicate his ability to work for reformation.

At the same time, Knox had no difficulty admiring men who held the office of bishop, as evidenced by his clear respect for Ridley, Latimer, and Cranmer. He includes them, after their martyrdom, on a list of the "most faithful servants and dear children of God." Even before their martyrdom, he had no difficulty working closely with reformers who held what he believed to be unbiblical offices in the Church. ". . . he acquiesced in the authority exercised by a part of the bishops, under the direction of the privy council, and endeavored to strengthen their hands in the advancement of the common cause, by painful preaching in the stations which were assigned to him. But he could not be induced to contradict or to conceal his fixed sentiments . . ."[62] Clearly, Knox was willing to speak his mind, but was no schismatic.

The fact that the office of bishop was unbiblical did not keep it from being a pastoral office. This is why Knox had strong views on how the bishops of the Roman church should have been occupying themselves. "For he that is appointed pastor, watchman, or preacher, if he feeds not with his whole power; if he warns and admonishes not when he sees the sword come; and if, in doctrine, he divides not the word righteously; the blood and souls of those that perish for lack of food, admonition, and doctrine, shall be required of his hand. If our horned and mitred bishops did understand and firmly believe this, I think they should be otherwise occupied than they have been this long time bypast."[63] In other words, the office of bishop was unbiblical, but Knox had greater patience with those men who at least knew what any kind of pastor should be about. Knox was unflattering when he compared the behavior of licentious churchmen of his day with the officials who ruled the Jews at the time of Christ. ". . . at the coming of

Christ Jesus, impiety was in highest degree amongst those that pretended most knowledge of God's will."[64]

Knox also had a high view of the sacraments of the Church. He objected to superstition, not because he despised the Lord's Supper, but rather because he knew how the Supper was truly to be reverenced. His objection was that "the end and use of a true sacrament are not considered, but rather the people are led to put their confidence in the bare ceremony."[65] At the same time, Knox wrote against the perfectionist sectarians who would reject any church that contained any imperfections. "This sort of men fall from the society of Christ's little flock, with contempt of his sacraments and holy ordinances by us truly ministered . . . [they] denying any true kirk to be where vices are known."[66] These men had begun with the reformers, but unfortunately had veered off into their own opinions.

> For thereby some, which began with us to follow God, to profess Christ Jesus and to abhor superstition, are declined from the sincerity and simplicity which is in Christ Jesus; and have separated themselves from the society and communion of their brethren, in sects damnable and most pernicious . . . [67]

As a good churchman, Knox loved and appreciated the historical Church, with all her blemishes, along with the fathers of the Church. In his treatise on prayer, Knox freely and easily quotes from Ambrose and Augustine, to good effect.[68] We should recall that the writings of Augustine and Jerome had drawn Knox, in part, to the Reformation. He, like them, wanted no part of schism.

PATIENCE

*T*IMES OF persecution can induce a feeling of complete helplessness. During such a time, men must be encouraged to remember God is sovereign over all, and that the prayers of the persecuted do not fall upon deaf ears. God does hear the cries of his saints, despite the appearances of any surrounding horrors.

> *First, I say, this is my hope, that a just vengeance shall be taken upon those bloodthirsty tyrants, by whom Christ Jesus in his members is now crucified among you . . . And therefore, beloved in the Lord, albeit you find your hearts sometimes assaulted with dolour, with grudging, or with some kind of desperation; yet despair not utterly; neither be you troubled above measure, as that Christ Jesus should never visit you again.* [69]

Knox urged those who might be tempted to murmur, or worse, to capitulate, to remember the greatness of their God in all *patience.* It was not enough simply to maintain the faith; Knox was urging them to do so with full contentment.

The author of Hebrews speaks in the same way; "For consider Him who endured such hostility from sinners against Himself, lest you become weary and discouraged in your souls. You have not yet resisted to bloodshed, striving against sin. And you have forgotten the exhortation which speaks to you as to sons: My son, do not despise the chastening of the Lord, nor be discouraged when you are rebuked by Him; for whom the Lord loves He chastens, and scourges every son whom He receives (Hebrews 12: 3–6)." The genuine Christian life has often provoked monstrous cruelties in opposition, but exhortations to maintain that life seem detached and abstract if we do not understand the context which made the exhortation so necessary.

When we moderns talk about contentment, it is often in the context of the stress of a difficult job, or the strains of marriage. Perhaps the demands of driving in heavy traffic are getting to us. This is one of the ironies of circumstance. Niggling distractions can be the cause of enormous discontent, but unbridled ferocity against the faithful can provide an occasion for their serenity.

Knox rowed as a galley slave for a year and a half, and knew the torments that were possible to the flesh. He knew the nature of the fire of Bloody Mary's persecution; he knew the nature of the tempest that had been unleashed. This was a time when the enemies of the gospel were not afraid to use fire and sword, and to use them enthusiastically. For one example, the Inquisition in the Netherlands was a time of monumental struggle. The duke of Alva boasted that in the space of five years, "he had delivered 18,600 heretics to the executioner."[70] In the struggle between the Netherlands and Spain, more

Christians were put to death for their faith than had suffered martyrdom in the first three centuries of the Church at the hands of the Roman emperors. This was a time when Christian women could sing a song of triumph while "the grave-digger was shoveling the earth upon their living faces."[71] The last day will reveal which psalms God gave them to sing. This is true patience; this is peace, which passes understanding, and it guards the heart and mind.

In France, the St. Bartholomew's Day massacre occurred in the last year of Knox's life. The estimated number of those slaughtered is between 10,000 and 70,000. Some of those martyred were members of the churches in France where Knox ministered. This travesty inflicted a deep wound on his already exhausted frame. He was weak, but still able to preach, and so he entered the pulpit with the remainder of his strength. He thundered the judgment and vengeance of heaven against the King of France, and charged the French ambassador to Scotland to tell his master that "sentence was pronounced against him in Scotland, that the divine vengeance would never depart from him, nor from his house, if repentance did not ensue; but his name would remain an execration to posterity, and none proceeding from his loins should enjoy his kingdom in peace."[72] Upon this treatment the ambassador complained about Knox, wanting the regent to silence the preacher. This refused, the French ambassador left Scotland. This gives us another strange illustration in the history of "intolerance." The kingdom of France had just butchered thousands upon thousands of her own citizens, and the ambassador of that country took offense when confronted with the matter. His thought was apparently that a man who preaches that way must be intolerant, and, therefore, a public hazard.

It was a bloody time in the history of the West, and throughout his life, Knox served as a faithful pastor for just such a time, exhorting his people constantly to suffer their lot patiently, to wait upon God, and to work for their deliverance by all lawful means. We must never forget that *this* was the context of the exhortations to patience, and this was their everlasting crown.

TRADITION

*A*s we have already seen, John Knox had a high view of the historical Church, and in no way did he seek a separation from that Church. Many modern Protestants believe that the Reformation was that time when their forefathers threw out all tradition, but this is not what they sought to do at all. Their intent was to measure and evaluate all traditions by the Word of God, and reject those that did not measure up. This means they were fully willing to keep those traditions that were in line with the Bible.

After all, the New Testament contains more teaching on tradition than Christ's fierce diatribe against ungodly traditions (Matthew 15:3). "Now I praise you, brethren, that you remember me in all things and keep the traditions just as I delivered them to you (1 Corinthians 11:2)." The fact that Paul requires the keeping of these traditions means that it is possible to neglect them. This charge of *neglect* is the charge brought by the early Protestants against Rome.

"Therefore, brethren, stand fast and hold the traditions which you were taught, whether by word or our epistle (2 Thessalonians 2:15)." Paul certainly mentions oral tradition alongside written tradition. The early Protestants did take, however, the necessary step of assuming that oral traditions could not fly in the face of the written traditions.

Tradition is inescapable. There is a story told of the modern Baptist pastor who said, with a twinkle in his eye, "We Baptists don't believe in tradition. It's contrary to our historic position." The question is never whether we shall have traditions, but rather which traditions we shall have. The reformers were not so foolish as to believe they were building a Church where each generation needed to rediscover everything done anew. Knox fully expected a Protestant and biblical tradition to develop. "True it is; but his ordinary means appointed by his eternal wisdom, to retain in memory his benefits and graces received, are nowise to be contemned. God commands you to teach your children his laws, statutes, and ceremonies, that they likewise may teach the same to the generations following."[73] Tradition is necessary, but it is equally necessary that the tradition be *biblical.*

The Protestant objection against Rome was not that they were keeping the traditions of the apostles, but rather that they *were not* keeping the traditions handed down to them. "Let not your bishops think that Augustine speaks for them, because he names the church. Let them read and understand that Augustine writes for that church which professes the truth, and does suffer persecution for the defense of the same . . ."[74] Knox knew that far more was involved in keeping a tradition than simply keeping the *name* of that tradition. Christ rebuked those ecclesiastical leaders of His day who were active in honoring deceased prophets, and went so far as to accuse them of believing that the only good prophet was a dead prophet (Matthew 23:29–30).

So Knox was not revolting against the history of the ancient Church, but was rather fighting in the name of that ancient Church, and on behalf of it. "No, no, my lords, so you cannot escape God's judgment. For if your bishops are proved to be no bishops, but deceitful thieves and ravening wolves (which I offer myself to prove by God's word, by law and councils, yea, by the judgment of all the godly learned from the primitive church to this day) . . ."[75] Knox understood that his adversaries represented a modern development in the Church, and he was happy to prove it—out of the Bible, or, if you please, out of the history of the Church. We have already noted his desire for a general council of the Church that could establish the Reformation throughout the entire Church.[76]

This was not an inconsistency in the first Protestants; it was their position. John Knox began his life as a Protestant indebted to some of the great thinkers and theologians of the early Church. As already mentioned, several of the early Church fathers played a key role in bringing Knox to his Protestant convictions.

> *Among the fathers of the Christian Church, Jerome and Augustine attracted his particular attention. By the writings of the former, he was led to the Scriptures as the only pure fountain of divine truth, and instructed in the utility of studying them in the original languages. In the works of the latter, he found religious sentiments very opposite to those taught in the Romish Church, who, while she retained his name as a saint in her calendar, had banished his doctrine, as heretical, from her pulpits.*[77]

If charged with smashing the ancient traditions of the Church, Knox would *not* have replied by saying that this was a good thing to do. Rather, he would have pled guilty to smashing some recent innovations and counterfeit traditions. This is something he would do as a lover of the teaching and examples of the apostles—a lover of the ancient traditions.

PATRIOT

*W*HEN GOD used Jehoiada the priest to establish
Jehoash on the throne of ancient Israel, the
response of the wicked Queen Athaliah was entirely predictable. "When she looked, there was the king standing by
a pillar according to custom; and the leaders and the trum-
peters were by the king. All the people of the land were
rejoicing and blowing trumpets. So Athaliah tore her
clothes and cried out, 'Treason! Treason!' (2 Kings 11:14)."
Those who have sought only God's best for their respective
nations, but have been accused of treachery and treason in
return, fill the history of the Church.

John Knox provides no exception to this general pattern,
and he frequently had to explain himself. "Let a thing here
be noted, that the prophet of God sometimes may teach treason against kings, and yet neither he nor such as obey the
word, spoken in the Lord's name by him, offend God."[78]
What Jehoiadah did most certainly was treason as far as
Athaliah was concerned, but this did not mean that it was

sinfully treasonous in the eyes of God. "But hereof be assured, that all is not lawful nor just that is statute by civil laws; neither yet is everything sin before God, which ungodly persons allege to be treason."[79] John Knox knew perfectly well that the civil magistrate commonly resisted his doctrine.

However, this did not make him a revolutionary, in the modern sense of the word. He did not advance these doctrines out of a desire to be seditious, or to raise tumults. He saw, in case after case, that the spiritual obstinacy of princes was often the great bane of their peoples. He opposed those princes because God required the opposition, and he also opposed them because he loved the people of the commonwealth, those threatened by the tyranny. "For a great difference there is betwix lawful obedience, and a fearful flattering of princes, or an unjust accomplishment of their desires in things which are required or devised for the destruction of a commonwealth."[80]

Knox was one with the early Protestants in standing for the rule of law. No one, whether king or prince, could declare himself to be above the law through some monarchical fiat. Whenever anyone in authority defied the law of God, it was foolishness to submit to him. "True it is, God has commanded kings to be obeyed; but likewise true it is, that in things which they commit against his glory . . . he has commanded no obedience, but rather he has approved, yea, and greatly rewarded, such as have opposed themselves to their ungodly commandments and blind rage . . ."[81] A fear of God drove this and so many other features of Knox's thinking. "I confess, indeed, that if our troubles come by man's tyranny, then the most sure and most easy way is to run to God for defence and aid. But let God appear to be our enemy, to be angry with us, and to have left us, how hard and difficult it is then to call for his grace . . ."[82]

Despite many modern notions to the contrary, constitutional liberties were not invented in 1776. As seen in Knox, and in many other medieval and reformational political thinkers, the tradition of limited monarchical authority is a very old one indeed. A writer contemporary to Knox, a French Huguenot writing anonymously, not only argues for limits on the power of the king, but does so through constant appeal to ancient constitutional liberties. Knowledge of liberties guaranteed by European constitutions saturates the book, *Vindiciae Contra Tyrannos,* and, though surprising to many, makes constant appeal to them.[83]

Knox had been instructed at the university by John Major, who in turn had "imbibed the sentiments concerning ecclesiastical polity, maintained by John Gerson and Peter D'Ailly, who so ably defended the decrees of the Council of Constance, and the liberties of the Gallican Church, against the advocates for the uncontrollable authority of the Sovereign Pontiff. He taught that a General Council was superior to the pope, and might judge, rebuke, restrain, and even depose him from his dignity; denied the temporal supremacy of the bishop of Rome, and his right to inaugurate or dethrone princes . . ."[84] This understanding of the polity of the Church transferred easily to the civil realm, and was not a new development or innovation.

Despite his view that the preacher should clearly and pointedly preach about those things in the civil realm which pertain to Christ's Church, Knox was clearly of the mind that, governmentally, church and state should be separate. This biblical separation of church and state is far removed from our modern notion, which takes it as the separation of biblical *morality* and state. "He was of the opinion that the clergy ought not to be entangled, and diverted from the duties of their office, by holding civil places: that the bishops should lay aside their secular titles and dignities . . ."[85] In other words, the civil government must be Christian, but it must not be run by clerics.

In all of this, Knox was not a dry academician or political theorist. He carried great love in his heart, not only for his native Scotland, but also for England where he had labored greatly for reformation. "But God I take to record in my conscience, that the troubles present (and appearing to be) in the realm of England are doubly more dolorous *[sorrowful]* unto my heart, than ever were the troubles of Scotland."[86] In this he was a true patriot—one who loved his people, but loved the gospel and laws of Christ more.

THEOLOGIAN

*R*EADING THE works of John Knox brings a refreshing surprise. Though he was a profoundly learned theologian, he wrote in a very pithy and approachable style, appealing to laymen and theologians alike. Since we too often have the assumption that profound theologians must necessarily write over most everyone's head, we might mistakenly assume that Knox was not an original thinker in the realm of theology. This would be a serious error.

His writing and speaking reflected his principles. Theology was, in his mind, essential to the right living of every man. "But as I never laboured to persuade any man in matters of religion (I take God to record in my conscience) except by the very simplicity and plain infallible truth of God's word."[87] As God's word is plain and straightforward, so should the writing of its teachers and doctors be. As the fellow said, Christ said to feed the sheep, not the giraffes.

The theological contributions made by Knox divide into two categories. In the first, he added his voice and the weight of his authority to those controverted doctrines that all the Reformers held against Rome. In the second category, he advanced beyond the insights of the other Reformers, although he did not differ with them concerning any central principle.

A good example of the former would be Knox's teaching on the subject of predestination. All the Reformed, Luther included, held very strongly to the doctrine of predestination. Many modern heirs of the Reformation want to think that this doctrine was an unfortunate peripheral subject that had tragically and unnecessarily found itself dragged into the center of the dispute. They want to be able to appreciate the Reformation without having to deal with what Calvin called the *decretum horribile*—predestination. When Luther debated Erasmus on the subject, he ended that debate with an important compliment.

> *Moreover, I give you hearty praise and commendation on this further account—that you alone, in contrast with all others, have attacked the real thing, that is, the essential issue. You have not wearied me with those extraneous issues about the Papacy, purgatory, indulgences and such like—trifles, rather than issues—in respect of which almost all to date have sought my blood . . . you, and you alone, have seen the hinge on which all turns, and aimed for the vital spot.* [88]

Knox was no exception to this common attitude among the Reformed. He wrote a lengthy treatise on the subject that was fully in accord with the sentiments of the other Reformers. [89] An anabaptist, probably Robert Cooke, had written anonymously against the doctrine of predestination, and Knox answered him in a lengthy reply. "If the Reformer cannot be said to have added much to what 'that singular instrument of Christ Jesus, John Calvin,' had already written, he shows much acuteness of and expertness both in reasoning and in the application of Scripture."[90] Cowan also points out several aspects of Knox's writing on this subject that are worth noting. First, he took scrupulous care to restate his opponent's argument in detail, and in his own words. He was an honest adversary. And secondly, he displays throughout a tender anxiety to convince his opponent—at one point he states that he would give his life in order to join his adversary "fully to Jesus Christ." Knox had no question that God must be understood to be fully *God.* Otherwise, everything sound in religion unravels. "For whosoever goes about to remove from God, either yet to call in doubt his wisdom and foreknowledge, his justice, power, mercy, goodness, or free election, goes about, so far as in them is, to destroy and call in doubt his whole Godhead."[91]

The important area where Knox was ahead of the other reformers was on the question of civil disobedience and resistance. This was no doubt the result of multiple factors—the insights of Knox, the violent heritage of Scotland, Knox's experiences with half measures in England, and the circumstances which had providentially developed in Scotland. However it developed, the result was a theological doctrine of political resistance, which has had a profound influence down to the present day—even when the source of the doctrine is not acknowledged. As Knox stated to the nobility of Scotland, "in the name of God, I require of you, that the cause of religion may be tried in your presence by the plain and simple word of God; that your bishops be compelled to desist from their tyranny . . ."[92] This is written to the "lesser magistrates," those who already had political power, but Knox takes another step, profound in its implications. He tells the commons of Scotland that they must answer to God on this point also. ". . . God, who requires no less of the subjects than of the rulers."[93]

The work of Knox resulted in one of a few nations brought under a fully reformed understanding of church polity and church/state relations. On the Continent, men like Calvin were able to put their doctrinal understanding into practice, but just had one city to work with. The same was true with other Reformers such as Zwingli, Bucer, or Bullinger. In England, numerous competing claims soon diluted the Reformation, resulting in an eclectic hash of assumptions and opinions, and in France, the Huguenots were eventually driven out. In Lutheran countries, like Germany, the doctrinal differences between the Lutherans and the Reformed were very pronounced on such cultural issues, but once the doctrine had been established in Scotland, it spread everywhere. I recently had the interesting experience of discovering that the Constitution of my own state solemnly declares that the people have the right to reform, alter, or abolish the government, for whatever reasons they might deem appropriate. Those words are the contribution of John Knox.

FRATERNITY

For a man of such great energy and strong convictions, and for all the controversies he was in, Knox maintained a remarkably collegial and catholic spirit. When Mary Tudor ascended the throne, she removed many Protestant clergymen from their positions of influence and power. Speaking to Winchester, one of Mary's henchmen, a bloody persecutor, Knox spoke this way in a letter about the evil that was being done to his brothers:

> But now, to your perpetual shame, you return to your vomit, and are become an open arch-Papist again. Furthermore, why seek you the blood of Thomas Cranmer, archbishop of Canterbury, of good father Hugh Latimer, and of that most learned and discreet man, Doctor Ridley, true bishop of London? Do you not consider, that the lenity, sincere doctrine, pure life, godly conversation, and discreet counsel of these three, are notably known in more realms than England?[94]

Here we can see that Knox had been an Anglican, if we may be permitted to speak this way. He was certainly a Puritan in the Anglican church (indeed, he was one of the founders of Anglican Puritanism), and this is why at the same time, he preached and ministered and served faithfully within the Anglican communion. He was in no way a separatist, and had a good fraternal relationship with the Protestants at the court.

He had worked as a chaplain to Edward, a pious king, but one who occupied what Knox understood to be an unscriptural office. Although Knox knew that the office was unscriptural (because no mortal man could be the head of the church as Edward was), he was willing to work for gradual reformation under the leadership of Cranmer. He would not take a living in that communion, or a bishopric, because to do so would bind his conscience personally. The Church of England was not yet reformed enough for Knox to consider taking a permanent pastorate in it, and given the circumstances, it was unlikely that it could become reformed according to the Word. Knox was foresighted enough to see that trouble was inevitable. Although the Protestants were in firm control at court, they could not remove the parochial clergy, who were utterly corrupt. They could not be removed because they were not principled; in order to keep their income, they would do anything. As Ryle observed, "There was no getting rid of these worthies, for they were ready to promise anything, sign anything, and swear anything, in order to keep their livings."[95] For Knox to take a permanent living would require him to make bricks without straw. He would be spiritually obligated to exercise discipline in the Church, but would not be able to do so.

We must however remember what he *was* willing to do, which was a considerable amount of reformational work within the Church. We have trouble understanding Knox at this point because we think when a doctrinal disagreement arises, we have only two options—separation and schism on the one hand, or total capitulation and compromise on the other. We must either leave, or cave, but Knox was of a different temper. He would not personally do what he believed to be unscriptural, but when he knew that genuine and sincere Christians differed with him on the point, he was more than willing to work together with them in every way that he could.

Knox certainly wanted to do more to reform the Church of England than was being done by the cautious Cranmer, and Knox had collided with the privy council over their offers of ecclesiastical positions to him, which he had refused on the grounds of principle mentioned above. Yet, he continued to labor faithfully for years in the Church of England until forced to flee because of persecution, and then, from the Continent, he wrote in strident defense of the godly Anglicans—his brothers Cranmer, Latimer, and Ridley. These last two men burned together, two true and noble bishops indeed. As their fire was kindled, Latimer spoke to Ridley, "Be of good comfort, Master Ridley, and play the man; we shall this day light such a candle, by God's grace, in England, as I trust shall never be put out."[96] Knox did not agree with them about the office of bishop, which office both Latimer and Ridley held, but Knox nevertheless called Ridley the true bishop of London. The fire of martyrdom burned all such disagreements away.

Given his ability to work together with men in true Christian charity when he had such strong disagreements with them, it is not surprising that Knox worked together very well with his associates in both Geneva and Scotland. Rows and fights did not characterize the work conducted by Knox and his co-laborers. Although circumstances often placed Knox in a place where he had to be alone, it would be wrong to characterize him as a loner. He believed strongly in the plural leadership of the Church, and he lived in a manner consistent with that conviction.

He was not a difficult man until someone decided to rebel against God—at which point Knox could be very difficult indeed.

VISION

*T*HROUGHOUT THE course of his life, John Knox was constantly oriented toward the future. He, more than most of his contemporaries, held the gift of ably analyzing the trajectories of current developments. Sometimes his warning that carefully crafted policies and stratagems were not going to achieve their intended result evidenced this gift. In other situations, he was not taken in by the professions of deceivers. On the positive side, he was able to see what would be necessary to maintain the achievements of the Reformation.

In classical literature, the tragic figure of Cassandra is notable. She had the gift of foretelling the future, but with this proviso—no one would ever believe her. Though this was not universally the case with Knox, it commonly was.

"During the time that Knox was in London, he had full opportunity for observing the state of the court; and the observations which he made filled his mind with the most anxious forebodings."[97] Part of the reason Knox did not attach himself in any permanent way to the Anglican church was his foresight of trouble on the horizon. Half-measures generally fall down half way. Knox was a man who believed that the law of God was consistent enough for us to plan and project according to it, even though exceptions might occur here and there. But as a general pattern, "Do not be deceived, God is not mocked; for whatever a man sows, that he will also reap (Galatians 6:7)."

This ability of his to see exactly what seed was planted gave him a great ability to predict what crop would grow. Part of the reason Knox became unpopular with subsequent generations was how he exercised this gift concerning Mary Queen of Scots. He was one of the few men whom she never fooled. This made him a very displeasing figure to her son, James I of England. James said that Buchanan, Moray, and Knox could not be defended "but by traitors and seditious theologues." Andrew Melville told the king that these men were the ones who had placed the crown upon his head when he was an infant, and that they deserved better of him. James then complained that Knox had spoken disrespectfully of his mother, to which one of the ministers of Edinburgh replied, "If a king or a queen be a murderer, why should they not be called so?"[98]

However, this remains a problem. "The greatest torrent of abuse, poured upon his character, has proceeded from those literary champions who have come forward to avenge the wrongs and vindicate the innocence of the peerless and immaculate Mary, Queen of Scots!"[99] Mary was a woman well-advanced in wickedness, and those who would defend her character, must necessarily assault those who in her day identified her character for what it was. In the front rank of such persons was John Knox, and so Knox, the man with clear vision, must be slandered as a blind and savage reviler of royalty. As McCrie noted, such defenders of the queen "have pronounced every person who spoke, wrote, or acted against that queen, to be a hypocrite or a villain. In the raving style of these writers, Knox was 'a fanatical incendiary—a holy savage—the son of violence and barbarism—the religious Sachem of religious Mohawks.'"[100] This is a heavy price to pay for having seen through that woman, and John Knox has certainly had to pay for it.

Nevertheless, his vision was clear and far-reaching in positive things as well. For example, he knew that ignorance, not learning, was the breeding ground for heresy and superstition, and so he was zealous to see schools established throughout the realm of Scotland. For this some who would ordinarily stand in opposition to Knox actually recognize and applaud him. As one of the first advocates of universal education, he sometimes wins grudging praise from some critics who see him (almost in spite of himself) as the father of the "universal" education we take for granted now.

Now it is true that he strongly urged the establishment of schools throughout the nation. "Now, last (omitting things of no less importance to your wisdoms), for the preservation of religion, it is most expedient that schools be universally erected in all cities and chief towns . . ."[101] These schools would have been established at the public expense, and so in one sense Knox could be seen as an advocate of "public schools," but two things about this must be noted.

First, the public support was to be applied from the monies that had previously belonged to the Roman Catholic churches. When the Roman church was disestablished in Scotland, the question naturally arose concerning what should be done with all her wealth and income. Knox argued for the establishment of livings for Protestant ministers and the building of schools. This was a return, in his mind, to the proper use of Church funds. In other words, Knox would have been appalled at our system of funding the schools.

This also relates to the second issue, which is the vast difference between public education and pluralistic education. The education envisioned by Knox would have been homogenous, explicitly Christian and Protestant, and supported by a portion of the tithes of the people. For the magistrate to pretend neutrality in all religious matters, as happens today, and to fund the schools through "secular" taxes would have been, for Knox, unthinkable. Knox would have identified pluralism for what it is, idolatry, and he would have had nothing to do with it. We would have in this rejection, once again, a good specimen of Knox's clear vision.

ZEAL

A FRIEND of mine once ironically defined a legalist as someone who loved God more than he did. We might alter the definition somewhat to make John Knox's indefatigable zeal a little less convicting to us. A zealot, a fanatic, is anyone who loves God and His Word in a way that embarrasses us.

It is not really possible to love God too much. It is not possible to take his Word to extremes, because His Word prohibits that use of it. If a man is careful to keep his conduct, motives, attitudes, and manner within the boundaries set by Scripture, how could we object to him without objecting at the same time to the Bible itself? If we really object to his behavior as Christians, we must do so because he was not conforming to the Scriptures in some way, and this means that the complaint is that he is not scrupulous *enough,* not that he has gone overboard. This is why Jesus said that unless the righteousness of His disciples exceeded that of the Pharisees they would by no means enter the kingdom of heaven (Matthew 5:20). The problem with the Pharisees was not that they were too righteous, but rather that they were hypocritical and unrighteous.

So we see a man who might certainly be extreme in the *name* of true religion, but this is a different thing altogether. Jesus warned of those who offered twisted service up to God in the name of God. "They will put you out of the synagogues; yes, the time is coming that whoever kills you will think that he offers God service (John 16:2)."

The key is to stay clearly within the confines established for us by the Word. The apostle Paul instructed us to be careful not to go beyond what is written. "Now these things, brethren, I have figuratively transferred to myself and Apollos for your sakes, that you may learn in us *not to think beyond what is written,* that none of you may be puffed up on behalf of one against the other (1 Corinthians 4:6)."

John Knox understood well that the Word of God need temper and restrain the zeal of men. "Let no man judge that I am more rigourous and severe in requiring that we abstain from all idolatry nor [than] necessity requires. No, brethren, I have learned always to contain and keep my affirmation within the bounds of God's scriptures."[102] This sense of restraint is what lay behind his emphasis on what has come to be called "the regulative principle of worship." His purpose in advocating this regulative principle was not to smother true zeal and piety, but rather to *channel* the zeal.

Righteous and reforming zeal filled John Knox, but he well knew the dangers of religious zeal. The apostle Paul had testified concerning the Jews of his day that they did have zeal. "For I bear them witness that they have a zeal for God, but not according to knowledge. For they being ignorant of God's righteousness, and seeking to establish their own righteousness, have not submitted to the righteousness of God (Romans 10:2–3)." This was the same problem in Knox's day. The Roman church certainly could not be accused of apathy; it was rather filled with a persecuting zeal—all in the name of Christ.

Knox shared with the Catholics an evident zeal, but he was distinguished from them in one notable respect—wisdom. He knew that all religious zeal had to be restrained by something outside a man, and that restraint had to be the plain Word of God, as it was written to us. In one of his earliest controversies, Knox said it this way; "All worshipping, honouring, or service invented by the brain of man in the religion of God, without his own express commandment, is idolatry."[103] The depth of his insight is really quite profound. Many modern Protestants see the doctrine of transubstantiation as idolatry because man worships a created thing (the host) as God—and some Protestants have trouble seeing even this. However, Knox did not identify this as the problem. This was certainly idolatrous fruit, but it was because it had grown up from an idolatrous *seed*—an invention of man in worship. Something that began in idolatry could not hope to end in true and pure worship. In this sense, Knox was a radical. The word *radical* comes from the Latin word *radix,* meaning root. Knox was concerned with the root of the matter, the root of all idolatries.

The Catholics were not the only ones who were attracted to their own inventions in worship. Knox was faithful in testifying against this error, even when committed by his own friends and co-laborers in the recovery of the gospel. His zeal was for the pure worship of God, and

God was the only One with the authority to determine what that pure worship should look like.

This was how John Knox saw that his zeal, and the zeal of all others, should be constrained. Anything done in the worship of God, in the name of Christ, should have His good authority for it.

PROVOCATION

*B*Y THIS time, the earlier descriptions of the kinder, gentler Knox may have so convinced some readers that they may be wondering where the common impression of him came from. Here is a man so tender and full of balanced love that they may have begun to wonder at how he possibly brought about any reformation at all. Where is the thundering Scot, the man who could make listeners tremble as they heard him preach? Where is the man who was a master of polemical invective?

This side of Knox was very real and very powerful, but before coming to that subject, we must remind ourselves of our true authority. We find the same thing in the pages of the New Testament. Jesus Christ, the one who suffered the little children to come unto Him, was also the one who identified the respected collections of theologians in His day as being little more than bags of snakes. And Paul, the one who wept over the enemies of the cross, was able to wish that they would complete the job of circumcision and castrate themselves. And John, one of the sons of thunder, lived up to his name when he excluded from the New Jerusalem all contemptible dogs. These scriptural examples of polemical writing do not contradict the biblical requirement of love; rather, they help to define it.

In this, as in so much else, Knox was a capable student. He had no use for the doctrine that taught that the elements of the Mass literally became the body and blood of Christ when the priest uttered the words of consecration. He dismissed it as "transubstantiation, the bird that the devil hatched by Pope Nicolas . . ."[104] Neither did he have any patience for indolence in the service of Christ. "But let all such belly-gods be whipped out of God's holy temple."[105] He did not spare his words when addressing the persecutors of Christ's Church. "I say, that now the devil rages in his obedient servants, wily Winchester, dreaming Durham, and bloody Bonner, with the rest of their bloody butcherly brood."[106] When he was speaking of the idolatry committed by the ancient Israelites, it has to be said that he did not really hold back. Moses, of course, took care of the problem. "Then he beat their calf to powder, and gave it [to] them to drink, to cause them [to] understand that their filthy guts should receive that which they worshipped for God."[107]

Speaking of a proud adversary at court, Knox dismissed him in this way. "And who, I pray you, ruled the roost in the court all this time, by stout courage and proudness of stomach, but Northumberland?"[108] When Knox came to discuss the work of Cranmer in the English reformation, he did not deal gently with Cranmer's enemies.

> [God] specially gave such strength to the pen of that
> reverend father in God, Thomas Cranmer, archbishop of

*Canterbury, to cut the knots of devilish sophistry linked
and knit by the devil's Gardiner (and his blind buzzards),
to hold the verity of God under bondage. . ."*[109]

Knox was not just provocative in his invective. His least
successful provocation—his view on women in government—was not written in inflammatory prose. *The First
Blast of the Trumpet Against the Monstrous Regiment of
Women* was plain and straightforward, but it was by no
means incendiary. The reaction it got, however, has made it
seem incendiary in retrospect. We must discuss the whole
affair in the context of the reign of Bloody Mary. Knox was
not afraid to attack Mary wholeheartedly and her "most
tyrannical iniquity"[110] and in doing so, he wanted to
employ every weapon at his disposal. The legitimacy of her
rule as a woman was one such weapon. This is not to say
that Knox argued pragmatically; he really held to this position. This should not be a surprise to us, because so did virtually all of Europe. "Knox's theory on the subject was not
novel."[111] France, a Catholic power, excluded women
from the throne by law. The work was embarrassing
"because in a certain sense nearly everyone (except regnant
queens) agreed with Knox. Everyone knew that it was
contrary to natural and divine law that women should
rule men."[112]

The problem came about because of this *agreement.*
No one in Europe was in a position to answer Knox with
the thundering confidence that Queen Elizabeth would
demand because everyone knew that Knox was right in his
position. The only defense possible for them was an appeal
to the fallenness of the world. And "no woman likes to have
her social position defended as one of the inevitable results
of the Fall."[113] So Knox was guilty of a tremendous *faux pas*

because he had put them all in this position, and the book certainly did hurt the Protestants. Calvin and Bullinger both agreed with the content of the book, but Calvin suppressed it at Geneva anyway because of its detriment to the Protestant cause. Calvin was certainly distressed at the damage caused, as he put it, by one inconsiderate and proud man. Calvin had a good practical point—Philip had not told the eunuch to depose Queen Candace.

In Knox's defense, Knox wrote the book against Mary, a virulent persecutor, but the year the book was published, Mary died, and so the book hit Elizabeth, who was not the kind of person to take such things kindly. None of this was Knox's intention. Knox was more than willing to accommodate himself to the necessities of the "fallen creation" with a Protestant queen, recognizing her as a Deborah raised up by God. However, none of this made Elizabeth happy. Knox's most successful provocation took on a life of its own and is still sighted from time to time in the literature of our feminist age.

CLARITY

*T*HE CURRENT and established wisdom commonly judges clear thinking to be a minor—albeit real—nuisance. All too often, an avalanche of human stupidities will bury an insightful man, and all because he would not acknowledge the force of the arguments!

Truth remains truth, however, for all that, and God in His providence has determined that certainly lonely individuals be assigned the duty of articulating the truth, despite the appearances. As Knox put it, "I shall be judged sharp; but be you admonished to flee all confederacy with that generation. For I speak and write in the presence of him before whose eyes the blood of his saints is so precious, that no worldly power was every found able to maintain long (or defend) such as delighted in the shedding of the same."[114] A certain type of man is always able to trim his sails to suit the prevailing winds, and he takes pride in the fact that he is adept at it. He does not know where he is going, but he is making good time. Because everything is proceeding so smoothly, he thinks a final reckoning will never come, but it does.

John Knox had the clarity of mind he did because of his grasp of what theologians call the antithesis. From the very beginning of our race, the seed of the woman and the seed of the serpent have been engaged in ultimate combat. One writer has called it constant, total war. According to the word of God, peace between the two is an utter impossibility, and the *appearance* of peace is simply the continuation of the war by other means.

Put another way, a fundamental difference exists between the righteous and the unrighteous, but for the temporizers and pragmatists of all ages, the difference is simply one of degree. The great theologian R.L. Dabney once commented on an effeminate form of American conservatism which would never be guilty of the "folly" of martyrdom, and which was simply the shadow that followed radicalism to perdition. This is the same phenomenon which caused one wit to observe that if the liberals in our Congress were to introduce a bill to burn down the Capitol, the conservatives would counter with a bill to phase the project in over the course of three years. When one group wants to drive us over a cliff at eighty miles an hour, it is hardly a pragmatic response to insist on fifty miles an hour. This is why "pragmatic" temporizers of all ages have never liked the discovery that pragmatism can be convicted by its own standard—it does not work. Nothing ruins a thriving party of consensus like being hosed down with the ice cold water of truth. And nothing makes the builders of consensus more unhappy. They want to build, but not with the materials given by God. "But vain it is to crave reformation of manners, where religion is corrupted."[115]

The great example of this mentality in Knox's time was William Maitland, a man of great abilities, as temporizers often are. Early in Knox's ministry in Scotland, Maitland took the moderate Protestant course. A question had arisen as to whether the Protestants were obligated to abandon attendance at the Mass. A debate was held between Knox and Maitland, and "Maitland defended the practice with all the ingenuity and learning for which he was distinguished; but his arguments were so satisfactorily answered by Knox, that he yielded the point as indefensible, and agreed, with the rest of his brethren, to abstain, for the future, from such temporising conduct."[116] This may be noted as the formal beginning of the Reformation in Scotland, since it resulted in separate observances of the Lord's Supper.

Although Maitland came to agree on this occasion, it is fair to say that temporizing was regularly his first instinct. After the return of Mary Queen of Scots, Maitland became the secretary of state. The general assemblies of the Church were an eyesore to the queen, and so her courtiers began to absent themselves from these assemblies. A dispute then arose over whether or not the Church could assemble without her majesty's leave. On this point, there was a sharp dispute between Knox and Maitland. Knox saw clearly, but Maitland, although a Protestant, did not. "Take from us the liberty of assemblies," Knox said, "and take from us the gospel."[117]

Later, when Knox was tried for treason on a trumped up charge, Maitland tried to persuade him to exhibit a timely submission to the queen's resentment. Knox would not bend—"he would never confess a fault when he was conscious of none."[118] Maitland was concerned at Knox's suicidal course, but Knox was acquitted on all charges— and the queen was utterly frustrated. It was yet another example of how Knox's lack of concern for success directly contributed to his success, and Maitland's pragmatic course would have led to disaster.

John Knox finished his course in honor and with integrity, and that course was one of no compromise. And William Maitland finally threw in his lot with the queen's faction and, like Kirkaldy, ended his life in ignominy, a defeated suicide.[119]

FAMILY

JOHN KNOX married twice, and had two sons from his first marriage and three daughters from his second. He was a kind husband and father, and appears to have been entirely happy in his household. John Calvin described his first wife, Marjory Knox, as *suavissima,* and said that she was a wife whose like cannot be found anywhere. She was certainly an impressive woman.[120] She was a very great help to Knox in the work he had undertaken, and he thought of her as his "most dear sister." Marjory's father had opposed this marriage.

> At this time it was judged proper by both parties to
> avow the connection, and to proceed to solemnize
> their union. This step was opposed by the young lady's
> father; and his opposition was accompanied with cir-
> cumstances which gave much distress to Mrs. Bowes
> and her daughter, as well as to Knox. His refusal seems
> to have proceeded from family pride; but there is

> *reason to think it was also influenced by religious*
> *considerations . . . he appears to have been, if not*
> *inclined to Popery in his judgment, at least resolved to*
> *comply with the religion now favored by the court.* [121]

Knox's two sons from this union were named Nathanael and Eleazar. Around 1566, they went to England, where their mother's relatives were living. They were educated at Cambridge, and both appeared to have died without issue. Nathanael obtained both a bachelor's and master's degree, and was made a fellow at Cambridge. He died in 1580, about eight years after his father died. Eleazar became a vicar in the Church of England, and lived until 1591.

His second wife was a young woman under the age of twenty named Margaret Stuart, related to the royal house. She was the daughter of Lord Ochiltree, a man who had stood by John Knox even when many others deserted him. She bore him three daughters, and although we do not know much about her, this was also a happy union. She ministered to him on his deathbed, reading passages to him at his request. "She continued to discharge the duties of a wife to him with the most pious and affectionate assiduity until the time of his death."[122] Knox had instructed her and his secretary to share the daily reading to him of the seventeenth chapter of John, Isaiah 53, and one chapter of the book of Ephesians, which they did until his death. After Knox's death, still a young woman, Margaret married Sir Andrew Ker, an ardent reformer.

John Knox had a high view of the responsibilities of fathers. "The only way to leave our children blessed and happy is to leave them rightly instructed in God's true religion . . . And therefore God straitly commands the fathers to teach their sons the laws, ceremonies, and rites . . . Then

God would that the life and conversation of the fathers should be a schoolmaster to the children . . . The chief schoolmasters (the Holy Ghost excepted) of the age follow-ing are the works, practices, and life of the forefathers."[123] In his discussion of family worship, Knox delivered a solemn charge. "No, brethren, you are ordained of God to rule your own houses in his true fear, and according to his word. Within your houses, I say, in some cases, you are bishops and kings; your wife, children, servants, and family are your bishopric and charge."[124]

John Knox certainly passed his commitment to the gospel on. His daughters were named Martha, Margaret, and Elizabeth. Martha married James Fleming, a minister in the Church of Scotland. Margaret married Zachary Pont, and the third daughter married John Welch, a courageous minister in Ayr. Welch was exiled for his opposition to King James, and they lived in France for sixteen years. There he gave himself so vigorously to the study of French that he was able to preach in fourteen weeks. He eventually lost his health, and his physicians told him his only prospect of recovering was to return home. Therefore, Elizabeth came back to England to seek liberty for her husband to return, and presented her petition at the court of James. The king asked who her father was. She replied, "John Knox." He exclaimed, "Knox and Welch! the devil never made such a match as that." "It's right like, sir," she said, "for we never speered [asked] his advice." The king finally told Elizabeth that her husband could return home if he would submit to the bishops. Mrs. Welch lifted up her apron, held it out toward the king, and said, "Please your majesty, I'd rather kep [receive] his head there."[125]

James had denied her request, but the spirit of Knox had certainly triumphed in his household.

Virtue

*T*HE CLERGY were not to consider religion an instrument of personal advancement. As far as John Knox was concerned, those clergy who pursued the ministry for the benefits it could bring to them were beneath contempt. Their approach was carnal, fleshly, like the false religion exhibited in the time of Christ.

> *But no part of this doctrine pleased them, or could enter into their hearts; but their whole mind was upon their bellies, for sufficing whereof they devised and imagined that they would appoint Christ Jesus to be their worldly king; for he had power to multiply bread at his pleasure.* [126]

Knox was greatly concerned to show that he did not minister as so many before him had done. In this he followed the example of the apostle Paul, who exhibited a zeal for his own defense as a faithful minister of Christ, while at the same time showing a humility in his clear understanding of his own frailties. When speaking with the elders of the church at Ephesus, Paul said this to them, "I have coveted no one's silver or gold or apparel. Yes, you yourselves know that these hands have provided for my necessities, and for those who were with me (Acts 20:33–34)." In his conduct of his ministry, he was above reproach and was not afraid to appeal to God and to those who had a close understanding of his ministry. Even so, at the end of his life, he still reckoned himself among the "chief of sinners (1 Timothy 1:15)." Such humility and confidence in tension is a characteristic of true Christian leaders.

In this sense, and with this qualification, Knox knew that he had lived in a virtuous way. "God is witness, and I refuse not your own judgments, how simply and uprightly I conversed and walked amongst you; though in his presence I was and am nothing but a mass of corruption, rebellion, and hypocrisy; yet as concerning you and the doctrine taught among you, as then I walked, so now do I write in the presence of him who only knows, and shall reveal the secrets of all hearts, that neither for fear did I spare to speak the simple truth unto you; neither for hope of worldly promotion, dignity, or honour, did I willingly adulterate any part of God's scriptures . . ."[127] In the sight of God, Knox knew himself to have fallen far short of the standard of God's holy law. He was worthy to approach God based upon Christ's imputed righteousness only. It is not uncommon for modern opponents of Knox to take some of his own self-accusations in the court of God's law, and use them in just the opposite way he intended, in the court of human reputation. For example, in a letter to his mother-in-law, he said, "In body you think I am no adulterer. Let so be, but the heart is infected with foul lusts, and it will lust although I lament ever so much." He went on to say, "I am no man-killer with my hands, but I help not my needy brother so liberally as I may and ought." In this way, John Knox knew that he was far worse than his pen could express.[128] This did not mean he was disqualified from ministry; it meant he understood the source of all true humility.

This is why Knox was concerned enough to vindicate his character, and his doctrine, from any malicious slanders that his adversaries may direct against it. He called God to witness, and it is significant that he could make the same kind of appeal that Paul had made—"I refuse not your own judgments."

So as men reckon blamelessness, Knox had lived as a minister of Christ should live, but this truth does not depend upon the testimony of Knox alone, nor would he want it to. "With his brethren in the ministry he lived in the utmost cordiality. We never read of the slightest variance between him and any of his colleagues. While he was dreaded and hated by the licentious and profane, whose vices he never spared, the religious and sober part of his countrymen felt a veneration for him, which was founded on his unblemished reputation, as well as his popular talents as a preacher. In private life, he was beloved and revered by his friends and domestics."[129]

Within the circle of his friends, he believed himself to be, as he described it, "churlish," and what he meant by this was his periodic difficulty pleasing and gratifying his friends as much as he would like to have done. No doubt, he considered this a sin on his part, and he asked his friends to excuse him for it. The problem was the result of periodic melancholy, but was not the cause of any dislocations in his relationships with those close to him. His friendships were "sincere, affectionate, and steady."[130]

He was a man who loved virtue in his private life, and by his ministry, he brought public virtue to Scotland. Before Knox brought "Calvinism" to Scotland, the people were ignorant, wretched, degraded in body and mind, and their morals were just as bad. One could accurately describe most Scots as filthy in their persons and in their homes, and exceedingly superstitious. Then "Knox made Calvinism the religion of Scotland, and Calvinism made Scotland the moral standard for the world."[131]

HATRED

NOX POSSESSED one important characteristic that many have difficulty understanding today. This is not surprising, given that this attribute was his ability to hate clearly. We live in a time when people interpret virtually *any* strong doctrinal conviction as hate. Of course, modern politicians like to inveigh against what they call "hate crimes" (as though love motivates other more mundane crimes).

The hatred that Knox bore toward all falsehood is one of the most obvious things about him, and on this issue, he consequently presents an easy target to modern critics. "He was a good summarizer of the accepted truth; but he was a savage hater, and obstinate defender of a position once he had adopted it."[132] In case anyone was wondering, being a "savage hater" is a bad thing. Or take this, from an issue of *Christian History,* purporting to honor Knox's contribution, "John Knox was a strange and rather frightening character. He was narrow-minded and intolerant. He lacked generosity of spirit and loved to hate."[133] Of course, this also carries the assumption that hatred is necessarily a failing of character.

Once again, we find ourselves running into Knox the biblicist. He was nothing if not committed to the Scriptures, and the Scriptures know nothing of our modern sentimentalist understanding of love, and the facile assumption that hatred must always be wicked. David was not afraid to say that God Himself hates all workers of iniquity (Psalm 5:5), and in another psalm he was not afraid to add his hatred to those who hated God (Psalm 139:21–22). Scripturally speaking, it is not enough to say that love and hate are opposites. Love of what? Hatred of what? Why? How?

The thing is not so simple. The Bible teaches us, for example, that love is a sin. "Do not love the world or the things in the world. If anyone loves the world, the love of the Father is not in him (1 John 2:15)." The Bible also teaches that hatred is a godly virtue. "But this you have, that you hate the deeds of the Nicolaitans, which I also hate (Revelation 2:6)."

Of course, as all Christians know, there is a type of hatred that is loathsome to God—in fact, He *hates* it. This is something which John Knox also knew, and which his modern critics miss. In a letter to persecuted saints, he makes certain essential distinctions, " . . . beloved brethren, you must avoid two things. The former, that you presume not to be revengers of your own cause, but that you resign over vengeance unto him who only is able to requite them, according to their malicious minds. Secondly, that you hate not with any carnal hatred these blind, cruel, and malicious tyrants; but that you learn of Christ to pray for your persecutors, lamenting and bewailing that the devil should so prevail against them, that headlong they should run, body

and soul, to perpetual perdition."[134] Knox goes on to show
that there is a scriptural and spiritual hatred, which is a
work of the Holy Spirit in the hearts of God's elect. In other
words, we may not hate in our own name, in our own
cause. We must, however, display a zeal for God's laws and
gospel, and take special care not to tangle this zeal up with
any of our own fleshly desires to "get even." Hatred must
be holy, according to Knox.

This is what Knox sought in his own life. "And here I
call my God to record that neither profit to myself, hatred
of any person or persons, nor affection or favour that I bear
towards any private man, causes me this day to speak as
you have heard; but only the obedience which I owe unto
God in [the] ministry, showing of his word, and the
common love which I bear to the salvation of all men."[135]
When he stood in the pulpit, he was not his own man, but
only an ambassador. This meant that if God declared his
hatred toward something, and that something was present
before the eyes of the preacher, he had an obligation to
speak against it in the name of Christ.

Of course, it was very easy to confound godly and
ungodly hatred during times of persecution. And so the
saints are to take care to pity those who persecute, and only
hate when it is the work of the Spirit of God, in full accordance with His Word. ". . . and so these tyrants are more to
be pitied and lamented, than either feared or hated—
except it be with a perfect hatred, which the Spirit of God
moves in the hearts of God's elect against the rebellious
contemners of his holy statutes; wherewith Jeremiah the
prophet was inflamed when that he prayed, 'Let me see thy
vengeance taken upon thy enemies, O Lord.'"[136]

The apostle Paul instructed the Romans that they must
not take vengeance, not because vengeance was wrong, but

rather because vengeance belongs to the Lord (Romans 12:19). Thus Knox had no difficulty calling upon the Lord to deliver "the hot vengeance of God"[137] against the cruel persecutors of Bloody Mary's reign. In this he was simply following the pattern set by the martyrs of the first century. "When He opened the fifth seal, I saw under the altar the souls of those who had been slain for the word of God and for the testimony which they held. And they cried with a loud voice, saying, 'How long, O Lord, holy and true, until You judge and avenge our blood on those who dwell on the earth (Revelation 6:9–10)?'" The only time the word *alleluia* is used in the New Testament occurs when the saints of God see the smoke ascending from the destruction of Babylon (Revelation 19:3).

The day of all great judgments will certainly come, and those saints who faced fire and sword for their love for Christ Jesus, including John Knox and his friends, will not be rebuked for their prayers. Rather, that is the time their prayers will be answered.

ORATOR

*A*S WE consider the life of Knox, one occasion for regret is the fact that he was a magnificent preacher, and we have only one of his sermons extant. The letters and books we have from his pen are quite valuable, but they do not really indicate what Knox represented to his generation. He was, first and last, a man who set the pulpit on fire. He was many things, and had many abilities, but the greatest of his abilities was his power of combining earthy and heavenly eloquence in the pulpit. The people of Scotland loved to hear him. "The truths which he discovered, he felt an irresistible impulse to impart to others for which he was qualified by a bold, fervid, and impetuous eloquence, singularly adapted to arrest the attention and govern the passions of a fierce and unpolished people."[138] As the common people of another era also discovered, it is possible to speak with authority and not like the scribes.

He did not believe at all in bland preaching. Judging from his expressions and turns of phrase in his published writings, we can only imagine how formidable he was when granted the only two weapons he ever desired—an open Bible in his hands, and the liberty to speak. "And, in this quarrelle, I present myself againste all the Papistes within the realme, desireing none other armore but Goddis holie word, and the libertie of my tonge."[139]

He preached like a controlled tornado, and was able to preach life into discouraged followers of the Reformation and fear into complacent sinners. Near the end of his life, he was still like to "ding the pulpit into blads," and could still cause one note-taker to stop because Knox made him tremble too much to write. He did not believe in bland preaching because the situation was too critical for such trifling. "In which, albeit I have not played the orator, dilating and decking the matter for the pleasure of itching and delicate ears, yet does my conscience bear me record, that with simplicity I have advertised you of a mortal danger . . ."[140]

This does not mean that Knox was an enemy to effective rhetoric; he knew what he was about, and he employed the arts of a good rhetorician most effectively. He was simply opposed to histrionic rhetoric, a fireworks display to no effect. As always, he aimed at the target. One of his most effective weapons in this was a biting wit, which he frequently used to dismiss the work of his adversaries' most imperfect wits. "And in which they glory as of most precious pearls, forged by their own brains, and polished by the finest of their wits . . ."[141]

Due to Knox's bluntness, his critics often accuse him of railing and sedition. Near the end of his life, Knox addressed this question.

> *Railing and sedition they are never able to prove in me,*
> *till that first they compel Isaiah, Jeremiah, Ezekiel,*
> *St. Paul, and others, to recant; of whom I have learned,*

plainly and boldly, to call wickedness by its own
terms—a fig, a fig, and a spade, a spade. [142]

The book of Proverbs tells us that an honest answer is like a kiss on the lips, and in Knox's day, an honest sermon had the same effect. The people knew they were getting the ungarbled word when they listened to this man.

This biblical and prophetic invective makes modern Christians a little nervous, but Knox would probably have something funny to say about that too. Our nervousness would certainly not slow him down any. James Beaton was more careful for the world "than he was to preach Christ . . . and as he sought the world, it fled him not."[143] Knox assailed the Abbot of Paisley for keeping a mistress, but then he also added, "how many wives and virgins he has had since that time in common, the world knows, albeit not all, and his bastard birds bear some witness."[144] John Sinclair, bishop of Brechin, was "blind of one eye in the body, but of both in his soul."[145] Lady Erskine was a "sweet morsel for the devil's mouth," and when Mary of Guise was made regent, the crown on her head was as unsightly as if men had thought to put a saddle on the back of an unruly cow.[146]

This was not mere name-calling. In his sermons, Knox coupled this pointed language, in deadly earnest, with most serious pleas to consider the claims of heaven, to abandon the inventions of the antichrist, and to come, and welcome, to Jesus Christ. In this, he was everything a Christian orator ought to be. If someone objected to Knox's oratory on the basis that it was somehow "unChristian," Knox was able to point to the places in Scripture where he learned to speak in this way. It would be difficult indeed to accuse Christ of being unChristlike.

If Knox's enemies accused him of speaking in a way that was counterproductive, Knox could simply point at how effective his sermons were in routing the enemy.

In this, John Knox met an ancient classical definition of a true rhetorician—a good man, skilled in the arts of persuasion.[147] He was a very great preacher indeed, although he might receive low marks in a modern homiletics class.

PROPHET

*A*N OLD cartoon in *Punch* shows some tourists in Scotland encountering John Knox for the first time. A Scottish cabby helpfully pointed out an historic landmark. "Yon's the house o' John Knox." The American says, "Wal, who was this John Knox, anyway?" The shocked response was, "Mon! Do ye no read yer Bible?"

John Knox strikes a prophetic figure, looking for all the world like a latter day Tishbite. The picture made even more complete when we read about some of his prophecies, but before we can discuss them, we have to take into account some current issues in the modern church. One of our theological debates is between cessationists and non-cessationists—respectively, those who believe that miraculous gifts like prophecy ceased after the apostolic era, and those who do not believe they ceased.

Those who follow in the theological tradition of John Knox, the Reformed and Presbyterian, are generally cessationists. Charismatic Christians are non-cessationists, and are sometimes surprised when they find out about John Knox's prophecies—Knox never having been anywhere close to Azusa Street. Now it is not our purpose to enter this particular debate here, but it is important to be aware of as we seek to understand the character of Knox, not to mention his heritage. Non-cessationists, of course, would see in Knox's prophecy examples of the gifts of the Spirit operating long after the apostolic era. Cessationists tend to explain Knox's prophecies the way Knox himself did, as one making predictions based upon God's general way of governing the world.

However, it is not as simple as these two choices. First, let us consider some of the prophecies. We should remember Wishart's declaration at his execution that Cardinal Beaton would be dead within a few days. Even before this, shortly before Wishart was betrayed, he encouraged his followers with this—"God shall send you comfort after me. This realm shall be illuminated with the light of Christ's Evangel, as clearly as ever was any realm since the days of the Apostles. The house of God shall be builded in it . . ."[148] The notable thing about this is Knox's comment in the margin—"Prophecy spoken by Master George Wishart." In *some* sense, Knox considered the statement prophetic.

Coming to Knox himself, we can count some of his prophecies as simply his uncanny ability to extrapolate future events from present circumstances. In a letter to those being persecuted by Bloody Mary, he says, "But what shall be the kind of their plagues, and whom God shall use to execute his wrath, I cannot say; but let it be sufficient that they shall not escape the punishment that is prepared, no more than Haman did the gallows that he made for Mordecai the Jew."[149] This is the way he frequently spoke.

Knox lived in a world where men reaped the way they sowed. He had great confidence in the scriptural principle, and spoke in specific terms of it many times. He defended himself against the charge that he was setting himself up for a prophet in this way:

> *Ye would know the groundis of my certitude. God grant that, hearing thame, ye may understand, and stedfastlie believe the same. My assurances are not the mervalles of Merlin, nor yit the dark sentences of prophane prophecies; but the plane truth of Godis word, the invincibill justice of the everlasting God, and the ordinarie course of his punismentis and plagis frome the beginning, are my assurance and groundis.* [150]

In other words, Knox knew how the world worked, and did not claim to have the prophetic powers of an Isaiah or Elijah. The very thought would have appalled him.

But we cannot explain all of his prophecies so easily. Once when he was a galley slave, their ship was off the coast of St. Andrews. Another prisoner asked him if he knew the place. "Yes, I know it well; for I see the steeple of that place where God first opened my mouth in public to his glory; and I am fully persuaded, how weak soever I now appear, that I shall not depart this life, till that my tongue shall glorify his godly name in the same place." [151] In other circumstances, he predicted the final victory of the Lords of the Congregation, when that outcome was gravely in doubt. After the death of James Stuart, a certain Thomas Maitland put a taunting (and unsigned) note in his pulpit. Knox read it, and showed no emotion, but near the end of his sermon said that there was one present who exulted over the death of a good man, and that this "wicked man, whosoever he be, shall not go unpunished and shall die where there shall be none to lament him."[152] As that man's sister noted, the ignoble death of her brother in Italy followed, with none to tend him. Knox specifically predicted the unhappy death of Kirkaldy of Grange as well. In all these instances, the predictions were *too* specific to be accounted for as though they were like the observation that people who eat too much get fat. Thomas McCrie, Knox's respected biographer, accounts for it as an extraordinary gift given in extraordinary times. He also recounts how Knox's contemporaries plainly took such things as prophecy. One could perhaps call this theory—punctuated cessationist.

Given the nature of these things, the evidence does not really support the notion that Knox delivered prophecies in the power of the Holy Spirit. At the same time, the deliverance was remarkable. What is left? One possibility at least. Part of the bane of modernity is that many of us have become materialistic in our assumptions about the world, and about what types of knowledge are possible to us *naturally.* My own view, which I can only suggest, is that Knox had genuine premonitions, which in fact came true. The world is a strange place. But he did not understand them as prophecies in the biblical sense, and did not see them as authenticating his ministry in any way.[153] And the fact that modern materialism does not leave room for such premonitions should not distress us at all.

INTEGRITY

*J*OHN KNOX was not in it for the money. He, along with virtually all the early reformers, hazarded everything he had for the sake of the gospel. Not only was he not in it for the money, he had nothing but contempt for those who were. The idea of trafficking in the truth filled him with disgust. "Neither yet would I recant (as they term it) one sentence of my former doctrine, for all the glory, riches, and rest that is in earth."[154]

The Reformation in Scotland was a genuine work of God. As such, it was not driven by economics—although economic issues certainly lay directly underneath. It would be more accurate to say that the Reformation began in part with revulsion over the moral and doctrinal corruption that wealth had brought to the Roman church in Scotland. In this sense, there was an economic factor in the Reformation from the beginning. In the same way, we could say that when Christ drove the moneychangers from the Temple, He was engaged in an activity, which had direct economic consequences. He did what He did because God's Temple was to be a house of prayer for all nations, and instead they had turned it into a pit of robbers. Therefore, we could call opposition to the idolatry of mammon an economic activity.

In a similar way, those who brought the Reformation about were willing to risk everything for the sake of it. Long before the days when the fruit of victory was apparent or certain, those in the vanguard had to declare themselves. Those who were making crude monetary decisions would not have taken those early risks. Once the Reformation had been established in Scotland, others gladly attached themselves to it—but these late arriving "merchants" were not those whom God had used to bring the great thing about.

> *Knox's unreserved self-dedication—at once devout and patriotic—to the Scottish Reformation stands out in fine relief, as compared with the self-seeking, or defective patriotism, which characterized not a few fellow-laborers in the cause. Protestant nobles reaped spoil from the Church's patrimony; Knox lived and died comparatively a poor man.* [155]

Even those who opposed him, despite what they might say, knew and understood him to be an honest opponent.

When Knox opposed such men over the patrimony of the Church, it was not because they were getting what Knox wanted for himself. Rather, Knox wanted the Church to use its revenues for the genuine work of the gospel—the support of ministers and schools and relief of the poor. The Church had long neglected its true work, and in Knox's thinking, the time for repentance had long passed. Those who pillaged the Church were able to do so because the

Church had not been fulfilling her mission, and so the losses were all hypothetical—lost opportunities. No one knew what a fruitful kirk would actually look like. Men knew what accumulated wealth in the Church looked like, and they wanted it transferred to their own coffers. Because Knox knew that Scripture alone sets the tasks of the Church, and not by political precedent, he was able to argue from principle on this issue in a way that few others understood.

We can see John Knox's commitment to integrity concerning money in other areas as well. When Knox was answering charges that he had not prayed for Mary Queen of Scots, he answered, "I am not bound to pray for her in this place, for sovereign to me she is not; and I let them understand that I am not a man of law that has my tongue to sell for silver, or favour of the world."[156] In words which foreshadowed one of the chief troubles of our own century, he grimly let it be known that he was a man of integrity—that he was not a lawyer. The redemption of Christ had purchased his tongue, and so Knox could not rent it out to those who might want to make some use of it.

Cotton Mather once spoke of a genuine dilemma faced by the people of God when he said that faithfulness begets prosperity, and the daughter devours the mother. God blesses obedience, and those blessings are often what choke out subsequent obedience. Rarely will followers of Christ set overt corruption as their goal; rather, they want to be conservative, consolidate gains, learn fiscal realism, and be "good stewards." Of course, nothing is wrong with good stewardship—other than the fact that it is a phrase which frequently stands in for bad stewardship. The Jews of the Old Testament were warned about this process, lest they say in their heart that *their* hand and *their* power had gotten them *their* wealth (Deuteronomy 8:17). It is a great dilemma, for faithfulness to God creates many potential idols.

At the end of his life, Knox was able to say, truly, "I profess, therefore, before God, and before his holy angels, that I never made merchandize of the sacred word of God."[157] With the apostle Paul, he refused to peddle the Word of God for profit.

FAULTS

*H*AGIOGRAPHY IS the practice of writing biographies of imaginary wart-free saints who never really joined the rest of us mortals in the wasteland of this world of ours. The book of Job tells us that man is born to trouble as the sparks fly upward, and that no man is without sin. These imaginary saints apparently walk two inches above the ground, never really touching down. Such glowing treatments are always a nuisance to those who love the truth, and they always set the stage for the *next* round of liars, the debunkers, those for whom the person in question could do no right.

In this book, I have had no desire to offer a hagiographic treatment of Knox's life. However, the man has been so slanderously reviled in so many ways, there is also danger in a dispassionate and even-handed treatment. His critics would quickly snatch up any acknowledgment of sin or fault and use it out of its necessary context, but the faults of John Knox were just those—faults of a man who loved and served Christ. We must not understand his faults as his enemies have sought to understand them, as indications of a deeply flawed or twisted human being, but this is what some want to do.

For example, Knox had rejoiced over the death of Mary of Guise because she had rejoiced over the corpses of the Protestant dead at Leith. One historian arbitrarily turns the whole thing around. "Such behavior is more characteristic of Knox himself than of the merciful Mary of Guise."[158] Apparently it does not matter who actually did this thing, what matters is who we think was most likely to have done it. Thus, we keep our prejudices secure.

Neither may we consider the option of the slanderous "compliment"—"Knox may not have been a good Christian, but he was good for Scotland." No. He was good for Scotland precisely because he was a conscientious Christian man. As friends of the truth he loved, we must understand that it is our task to understand his failings in their proper context.

John Calvin was a friend of Knox, and knew both his strengths and weaknesses. He knew that Knox was a man of unshakeable integrity, and that with this integrity he faced corresponding temptations. In 1561, Calvin wrote to Knox, "With regard to ceremonies, I trust, even should you displease many, that you will *moderate your rigour.* Of course it is your duty to see that the church is purged of all defilements which flow from error and superstition . . ."[159] Once Knox had seen and understood the truth, his temptation was to be too rigorous, as Calvin well knew.

He was a passionate man. "His passions were strong; he felt with the utmost keenness on every subject which interested him; and as he felt he expressed himself, without disguise and without affectation. The warmth of his zeal was apt to betray him into intemperate language."[160] He had a way of angering some, even when his position was entirely reasonable. The fact that those angered were frequently those who covered over their unreasonable tyrannies with soft words complicates the picture further.

Knox had true independence of mind, and this could easily be taken for haughtiness or disdain. Once he had settled on a position, dislodging him from it was extraordinarily difficult. He had the ability to "back off" his advocacy of a position, as he did with his teaching on the "regiment of women," but nothing would make him disavow it when he believed it to be right. This is apparent when he wrote to Elizabeth concerning his *Monstrous Regiment;* of course he was not "myndit to retract or call back" a word of it.[161] However, he was quite prepared to acknowledge Elizabeth as an exception, but Elizabeth, in reality the unreasonable one, never could bring herself to appreciate his little book. In short, even when he was not pressing a point, Knox could look like he was.

In one notable instance, he allowed himself to suggest a course of action that was not consistent with his general pattern of honesty. At one point in the civil struggle for the control of Scotland, when help from England was critical, and when England was reluctant to give it, Knox engaged in a bit of political intrigue that was really not worthy of him. Knox had always preferred the open and honest policy of clear opposition to the Catholic powers, but Elizabeth of England was reluctant to provoke France by helping the Scots Protestants. The Scots were in desperate need of help, and so Knox suggested that they could send a thousand men, but then disavow them as rebels. Sir James Croft replied to him that they could not do this without breach of treaty and dishonor, and Knox wrote back, apologizing for his "unreasonable request."[162]

Many extenuating circumstances surrounded this uncharacteristic lapse of honesty, but to emphasize those would only perpetuate the problem. The suggestion offered by Knox was a dishonorable one, and we are most like Knox at his best when we say so, straight on.

DEATH

*I*T IS extremely difficult to die well if you have not
lived well. Rarely do men rise to the occasion, contrary to how they have trained themselves to respond
throughout their lives. Christ said that the one who is faithful in little will be faithful in much, and nowhere is this
more plain than when men come to die. Because we moderns are not well-trained in our discipleship of living, it
should be no surprise that we do not die well. We have
many drugs to ease the pain for us, but unfortunately, these
drugs will often blur the mind, and we readily forget that
dying is our last act of earthly discipleship. The literature of
previous Christian eras reveals this understanding, an
understanding that is largely gone in our day. This is very
evident when we consider how the friends of Knox urged
him on to greater and greater faithfulness as he neared the
finish line.

Knox entered his last sickness on the 11th of November,
1572, seized with a severe fit of coughing. It had been his

practice through his life to read daily a few chapters from both Old and New Testaments, along with enough of the Psalms to finish that book of the Bible once a month. A few days into his sickness, it became apparent that he could not continue this practice, and so he set a course of reading for his wife and servant to share. Scarcely an hour passed during his last sickness when someone did not read some portion of the Scriptures to him.

On the 15th, two of his closest friends, John Durie and Achibald Steward, came to visit. They saw how sick he was and tried to leave, but he insisted they remain and eat with him. He got up for the last time, ordered a hogshead of wine, and spent the time at the table with them in a great deal of hilarity. It was the last time he was able to get up.

In his last statements, he was careful to address those subjects where there was great need. Like a true minister of Christ, he was not afraid to defend himself to the extent the cause of Christ was bound up in his person. He said, with the full knowledge that he was about to meet Christ:

> *I know that many have frequently complained, and do still loudly complain, of my too great severity; but God knows that my mind was always void of hatred to the persons of those against whom I thundered the severest judgments . . . I profess, therefore, before God, and before his holy angels, that I never made merchandise of the sacred word of God, never studied to please men, never indulged my own private passions or those of others, but faithfully distributed the talents intrusted to me for the edification of the church over which I watched.*[163]

His last day was the 24th of November. One of his friends, Kinyeancleugh, asked him if he was in any pain. "It is no painful pain, but such a pain as shall soon I trust, put end to the battle. I must leave the care of my wife and children to you, to whom you must be husband in my room."[164] That afternoon, one of his eyes failed and his speech was affected. He asked his wife to read the fifteenth chapter of 1 Corinthians. When she was done, he said, "Is not that a comfortable chapter?" Later that afternoon he said again to his wife, "Go, read where I cast my first anchor," upon which she turned to the seventeenth chapter of John, the place which had apparently been influential in his conversion.

He fell into sleep, punctuated with many moans. When he awoke, his caretakers asked him the reason for the moaning. He replied that during his life he had withstood many assaults from Satan, but they had been the kind of temptation which either led him to despair or to the allurements of the world. Now, he said, Satan had attacked him by suggesting that he had somehow "merited heaven and eternal blessedness by the faithful discharge of [his] ministry." He was grateful; God enabled him to resist here as well, and pressed on his mind the fact that he had *nothing* that God had not given him.

At ten that evening, they read the evening prayer. When they were done, another friend present, Dr. Preston, asked him if he had heard the prayers. He replied, "Would to God that you and all men had heard them as I have heard them; I praise God for that heavenly sound."

Around eleven o' clock, he sighed deeply, and said, "Now it is come." His servant Bannatyne drew near immediately, and urged him to think upon the promises given by the Savior, the promises that he had so frequently preached to others. When he saw that Knox was speechless, he asked him to give them a sign that he heard them, and that he died at peace with God. At this, he lifted up one of his hands, and went to be with the Lord.

He was not yet sixty years old, but had plainly worn himself out in his service to his master. He died as he had lived, the servant of another.

GREATNESS

*J*OHN KNOX is a towering figure in Scottish history, and a significant figure in world history. How did this come about? Like Calvin, he held no political office, and did not hold in his hands the reins of what we call power. In the office he did hold, he was simply a minister of the Word. However, this does not account for it, because we cannot duplicate the results of his ministry simply by ordaining ministers, even qualified and trained ministers. God is sovereign in all His works, and He alone can work the extraordinary. This is why men like Knox cause us to reconsider whether we have an adequate "theology of greatness."

The kind of greatness exhibited by Knox is simply inexplicable apart from the Spirit of God. Throughout the history of the Church, we see that God governs and advances His cause through the ordinary work of ordinary officers—elders, deacons, and ministers. We do not disparage the ordinary courses of our river at all, but the Church sometimes reaches flood stage, overflows her banks, and inundates all the surrounding country. This is because an ordinary office can be held by an extraordinary man, and the office cannot contain the work of God within that man.

We see throughout Scripture that the Spirit was often poured out in extraordinary measure on certain men to equip them to perform great tasks. The Spirit of the Lord came upon Saul, enabling him to be the first king of all Israel. He, by his disobedience, forfeited this blessing of the Spirit, and his dynasty crumbled. David, in his sin with Bathsheba, knew that he had forfeited God's blessing on the reign of his house in just the same way, which is why he prayed, "Do not take your Holy Spirit from me (Psalm 51:11)."

When God established Solomon on the throne of Israel, he bestowed upon him an extraordinary majesty. "So the LORD exalted Solomon exceedingly in the sight of all Israel, and bestowed on him such royal majesty as had not been on any king before him in Israel (1 Chronicles 29:25)." It was this "royal majesty" which enabled him to govern, and it was the gift from the hand of God.

We see the same kind of thing in the narratives of the early Church. The apostles were office holders of the apostolic office, and yet they were told to wait for the power from on high. We see the servants of God laboring in the first century under all the ordinary limitations of men, and we also periodically see extraordinary visitations of the Spirit, empowering them to speak the Word with great boldness.

This is the kind of testimony we have concerning the historic figure of John Knox—a great man in the hand of God. "A certain heroic confidence, and assurance of ultimate success, have often been displayed by those whom

Providence has raised up to achieve great revolutions in the world; by which they have been borne up under discouragement which would have overwhelmed men of ordinary spirits, and emboldened to face dangers from which others would have shrunk appalled. Knox possessed no inconsiderable portion of that enthusiastic heroism which was so conspicuous in the German reformer."[165] The Spirit of God cannot be upon someone to this extent, without them being aware of it. A great man may be aware of his greatness without megalomania—provided he understands the entire sovereignty of God.

His servant Bannatyne spoke of Knox's greatness after he had died, in an entry in his "Journal."

> *What dexterity in teaching, boldness in reproving, and hatred of wickedness was in him, my ignorant dulness is not able to declare, which if I should preis [labor] to set out, it were as one who lights a candle to let men see the sun; seeing all his virtues are better known and notified to the world a thousand-fold than I am able to express.* [166]

Bannatyne did not defend his master because his greatness was in question, but rather because his greatness made it necessary for his enemies to slander him.

The Spirit of God can make the donkey rebuke the prophet, but the Spirit of God can also fall on a man of strong natural talents. "That [Knox] possessed strong natural talents is unquestionable. Inquisitive, ardent, acute; vigorous and bold in his conceptions . . . He united, in a high degree, the love of study, with a disposition to active employment."[167] Knox was talented enough that if someone wanted to reject the idea that God's blessing was upon him, it would at least be superficially plausible to credit Knox himself with what was accomplished. However, this would require us to discredit the testimony of all those who knew the most about the source of his greatness. His greatness was in God.

He was a great man indeed, ideally fashioned by an all-wise God for his time. "Before the Reformation, superstition, shielded by ignorance, and armed with power, governed with gigantic sway. Men of mild spirits, and of gentle manners, would have been as unfit for taking the field away from this enemy, as a dwarf or a child for encountering a giant . . . Viewing his character in this light, those who cannot regard him as an amiable man, may, without hesitation, pronounce him a Great Reformer."[168]

PART 3
THE LEGACY OF JOHN KNOX

*But in all things I wish your eyes to be single, beholding only
in your enterprise the glory of God, your duty, and
the salvation of your brethren.*

—John Knox

*Now, if you be powers ordained by God (and that I hope
all men will grant), then, by the plain words of the apostle, is the
sword given unto you by God, for maintenance
of the innocent, and for punishment of malefactors.*

—John Knox

RECOVERING OUR HISTORY

*W*E HAVE a tendency to think that "forgetting" is a reasonable excuse for failure. Children who were told to do something often defend themselves for their lack of obedience by saying, "But, Mom, I *forgot.*" Rarely will the mother thank the child for confessing this additional sin and then administer another spanking. This is because we persist in thinking that "forgetting" ameliorates an offense. But this is not necessarily the case.

Throughout Scripture, forgetfulness is shown to be a very great sin in its own right. "They did not keep the covenant of God; they refused to walk in His law, *and forgot His works* and His wonders that He had shown them (Psalm 78:10–11)." Another psalm speaks in the same way. *"They soon forgot* His works; they did not wait for His counsel . . . *they forgot* God their Savior, who had done great things in Egypt (Psalm 106:13,21)." Jeremiah rebukes the people of God—". . . as their fathers *forgot* My name for Baal (Jeremiah 23:27)." The prophet Hosea makes the same point. "When they had pasture, they were filled; they were filled and their heart was exalted; therefore *they forgot Me* (Hosea 13:6)."

God has been very kind to our nation in many respects, and like a spoiled child taking virtually everything for granted, we have forgotten His kindness. One of God's great instruments for blessing us was the ministry and life of John Knox. We owe an enormous debt to him. The debt is not one we can really pay, except through remembering, and we have failed even to do this. Knox knew that his contribution to Scotland would have to be recognized eventually, but he could not have known how many other nations would benefit from his sacrifices. Of Scotland he said, "What I have been to my country, albeit this unthankful age will not know, yet the ages to come will be compelled to bear witness to the truth."[1] But that was Scotland; this is America. What's the point? Too often we will not see what Knox could not have helped but see.

The point is our forgetfulness. Knox could not have seen the future, but we are able to study the past. To this day we enjoy enormous blessings, both civil and ecclesiastical, and we have received them through the instrumentality of John Knox. First, how did we come to receive them, and then, what have we received?

Knox was used, of course, to establish the Reformation in Scotland, and he made an indelible imprint on the Scots' character. In a very real sense, he is the father of that nation. Several centuries after Knox, the revolt of Bonnie Prince Charlie was utterly crushed by the English House of Hanover. We might be more familiar with one of the representatives of that House, notably King George III. After the abortive revolt was put down, the English instituted a policy of stern repression in Scotland, and many of the adult men left that country. This particular repression was just one of the reasons the Scots (and the Ulster Scots) had to emigrate in the first half of the eighteenth century. For the most part, they came to America. In the first part of the eighteenth century, "a body of about 600,000 Scots was thus brought from Ulster and from Scotland to the American colonies, making about one-fourth of our population at the time of the Revolution."[2] One of these refugees was a Presbyterian clergyman named John Witherspoon. He taught at Princeton, and was an instructor to many of our founding fathers—he taught one president, one vice-president, ten cabinet officers, twenty-one senators, thirty-nine congressmen, and twelve governors. He was a signer of the *Declaration of Independence,* and may himself have been a descendant of John Knox.[3]

This stream of refugees was covenantally and theologically homogenous. In effect, they were all disciples of Knox. This is just one reason why we can agree with Douglas Kelly, who said, "The peculiar approach of Reformed Scotland to God, church, and civil government was a major stage in the development of modern political systems in the West."[4] The American War for Independence was overwhelmingly a Presbyterian conflict, and in many respects this war against the English was a clear continuation of the Scottish wars against the English.

What blessings did we receive from this? Before enumerating these blessings, it should be noted that our contemporary erosions do not remove the historical fact of these blessings, and only serves to remind us of our duty to remember before they are all gone. Representative government was one blessing. Again, Kelly. "This concept of power flowing upwards rather than downwards was to have immense influence in the development of the American mind, both in its religious and civil aspects"[5] Kelly is referring to the original character of our republic in its representative aspect. While greatly polluted in recent years, the tradition runs deep and can still be recovered.

Another part of the heritage is that of "covenantal thinking," where the rulers can be held accountable directly by the people as they discharge their duties under the limitations of a transcendent law. Even our term "federal government" comes from the Latin word for covenant—*foedus*. The feds do not function covenantally now, but that is our sin—we have forgotten.

A third blessing is the independence of the Church from the state. This does not mean, as it has recently been twisted to mean, the separation of biblical morality and state. But it does mean that the Church has been established by Christ, and is not a corporation of the civil magistrate. This consequently means the magistrate does not have the authority to interfere with the Church as she discharges her obligations before the Lord. This is what lies behind the phrase in the First Amendment, where Congress is told it may not interfere with the "free exercise" of Christianity.

Few American Christians today study history, and among those who do, they rarely go back past 1776. But we must do better than this. We must recover our heritage. And this means, in part, a recovery of the teaching of John Knox.

Rarely in One Man

*I*T WOULD be too easy to study Knox in a fragmented or piecemeal fashion. He was a man of such great abilities that it would not be hard to isolate just a few of those abilities and think the job was done. But consider his life again and reflect on some of what we have seen. John Knox was a preacher, teacher, pastor, theologian, political theorist and advisor, military advisor, scholar, constitutionalist, and very much a man of action. He conducted himself throughout these varied activities with honesty and integrity, very much able to comfort the afflicted and afflict the comfortable. He was loving, reverent, courageous, humble, balanced, severe, zealous, tender, and prophetic. In short, he was the kind of man who rarely walks across the world's stage. We are not likely to see someone like him again any time soon.

In some respects, this is inspiring, and in other respects, it can be discouraging. We are always inspired at the recounting of great deeds, and this is as it should be. John

Knox is no longer with us, but the God he served most certainly is. However, we can be discouraged the next moment because we forget what is involved in this—it can be easy to think that nothing can really be done against the forces of unbelieving modernity that we confront day after day. We need someone like Knox, we think, and waiting for *that* is like waiting for lightning to strike.

Hamlet noted that there is a purpose that shapes our ends, rough-hew them how we will. There is a purpose and plan behind all things (Romans 8:28), and the Lord of history plans a perfect correspondence between the various stages of history and the particular servants assigned to live in those times. And this includes the varied abilities of those servants. Knox did not serve a generic God; he served the God of battles. This God, this Lord of hosts, knows how to marshal His forces perfectly, and how and when to place his soldiers in every battle. Knox served a God who countless times had seemed to have all but abandoned His people, but Who then arose and scattered all His enemies. And so we should know by now that God does not intend to lose this war, although tired foot soldiers sometimes think He does.

If we were placing the troops in the battleline, we would assign Knox to our day. We need him desperately, we think. But apparently not—if we needed him to accomplish God's purposes here and now, we would have him. The lesson to draw from the life of Knox is not that every generation needs men just like him, and that in spite of this need, God, for reasons known only to Himself, persists on giving such men infrequently. Rather, the genuine lesson is that God does what He pleases for His greatest glory.

Scotland in the sixteenth century was a stark and brutal place. It was a spiritual wasteland. In many ways, the situation was far worse than the one we confront today. And in their situation, God supplied their need. But even under those circumstances, He did not arrange all the affairs as man might have wished. Why was a man of Knox's abilities sent to row in the French galleys for nineteen months? It was not because God thought the French needed some additional help in moving their ships around. Rather, He was shaping and molding Knox for what he would have to endure. God is in His heaven; He does whatever He pleases.

It has been well said that the kingdom of God advances through a series of glorious victories cleverly disguised as disasters. Nowhere is this more apparent than in the crucifixion of Jesus Christ, the downfall of Satan implemented by Satan. "But we speak the wisdom of God in a mystery, the hidden wisdom which God ordained before the ages for our glory, which none of the rulers of this age knew; for had they known, they would not have crucified the Lord of glory (1 Corinthians 2:7–8)." God's strategy was inscrutable in the first century, although we see the purpose of it now. His plan was inscrutable in the sixteenth century, although we marvel at His wisdom and graciousness now. But still we complain—what is God doing *now?*

The lessons to draw from the life of Knox have more to do with glorifying God for His wisdom in that life, and little to do with experiments toward some sort of reformation reenactment. Knox would not want us to glorify him, but rather to give thanks to God for whatever blessing he had brought. We should then look for an appropriate blessing for ourselves, in accordance with the greatness of God's wisdom.

As we remember this, we also must recall the fact that the enemies of God have taken notice of Knox as well. They assail him; we thank God for him. He was a frail bit of flesh, in whom God placed many strengths and graces. We do not despise the instrument, for God's strength is always made perfect in weakness.

So we honor a most unusual man, and we honor him *without jealousy.* He was a man in whom so many virtues came together that it is difficult to recount them all. He was an extraordinary man, whose greatness cannot be disputed by any. His personality was overpowering, and his zeal was utterly dauntless. His honesty could not be questioned, and his moral zeal and earnestness was tempered with a very earthy sense of humor. He was an idealist, but not a fanatical enthusiast. His station in life was that of a preacher, but through the force of his preaching, he made himself a potent force to be reckoned with in Scotland not only during his lifetime, but also for generations to come.[6]

LEGACY OF TRUTH

*O*NE TIME when he was speaking of the history of Israel, Knox drew a parallel to the soft counselors in the time of Bloody Mary. "They healed the sores and botches of the people, princes, and governors, with unprofitable plasters, and laid soft pillows under the heads of such as slept securely in all iniquity."[7] John Knox did not ever have a high opinion of those who soft-pedaled the truth. And this makes him an awkward, angular figure.

We cannot discuss the life of Knox with pretended neutrality. Either we are with him, or we are with the papists. But we do not call Roman Catholics papists nowadays, and the point is not the polemical style of the Reformation. Differences over matters of style would probably not have been of great concern to Knox. Rather, the issue is the theological *substance* of the Reformation. Either we agree with Knox that the Word of God is the absolute authority on all such matters, or we do not agree.

The legacy of Knox cannot be appropriated dishonestly or in ignorance. Too many modern Protestants have no idea what the early Protestants stood for, and yet they want to honor them as great reformers. But what did they reform, and how did they do it? No use looking *too* closely into such questions, we mutter. Not surprisingly, we discover that many modern Protestants are not historic Protestants at all, but have quietly adopted the basic theology of the Roman Catholic church, while avoiding Roman customs on peripheral matters.

I have not written this book in order to offend Roman Catholic readers, or Protestants either, for that matter. But in discussing history, a moment comes when one has to make a decision, a judgment call. In studying the War Between the States, was the South right? Or wrong? In studying the American War for Independence, did Romans 13 require the colonists to submit to the usurpations of Parliament? Or not? In writing this book, I must either appreciate Knox or attack him. He lived his life in such a way as to leave a biographer no other option.

The consequences of the Protestant Reformation are very much with us today. This means that we have a moral duty to answer the question which a reasonable Roman Catholic might pose to us—"Was the Reformation necessary, or was it the sin of schism?" If we answer that it was necessary, we had better understand the case our fathers made for it. If we answer that it was not necessary, and that it was the sin of schism, then we should repent and return to Rome.

Jesus spoke of the sin of honoring prophets outwardly in name, when the secret reason we honor them is because they are dead and cannot bother us. We honor them because they were kind enough to rebuke our disobedient ancestors instead of plaguing us. If we are to avoid this sin, and if we are to honor Knox in substance, and not just in name, we must know what our Protestant fathers stood for. A good summary of the Reformation truth they fought for has come to be referred to as the "five solas."

> Sola Scriptura: *This was the doctrine that the Bible alone, excluding the Apocrypha, was the ultimate and infallible authority in all matters of faith and practice. Other authorities were acknowledged, such as the Church, but these did not have infallible or ultimate authority. They could err, and there could be appeal beyond them to the final court of Scripture. By this, the Reformers did not mean what might be called "solo Scriptura," or an individualistic "just-me-and-my-Bible" approach. They had a high respect for the traditions of the Church, but did not believe them to be beyond correction.*

> Soli Deo Gloria: *All things, great and small, are to be done to the glory of God alone. The final purpose of all things is the glory of God, and, as the Westminster Shorter Catechism put it, the chief end of man was therefore to glorify God and enjoy Him forever. This includes the final purpose behind our salvation.*

> Solus Cristus: *There is only one mediator between God and man, the man Christ Jesus. We are not in need of any other intercessors as we come before the presence of God, whether they are angels, apostles, saints, or our Lord's dear mother.*

Sola Gratia: *Salvation is by God's grace alone, and does not come about through any kind of cooperation with our choices. Sheer grace is the only active power in salvation and leaves nothing to human choices or works. And it follows from this necessarily that salvation is not of him who wills, or of him who runs, but of God who shows mercy.*

Sola Fide: *The instrument that God uses to save a man is faith, and faith alone. God does not save because of that faith, but rather through that faith as it applies the merits of Christ's righteousness to the sinner. In other words, faith is the instrument of salvation, and not the ground of it. Faith is therefore seen as a gift of God, so that no one can boast.*

Now some of these issues may be hard for modern evangelicals to understand, because we are not accustomed to think in these categories. But if we understand and embrace them, then we are holding to the legacy of Knox. If we do not, however sincere we might be, we are squandering that legacy while retaining the name of it. This may make us uncomfortable, but Knox did not live his life with our comfort in mind.

GIVE US MEN

SPEAKING OF ancient Israel, Knox once spoke of their spiritual decline in this way: "Finally, the pastors were become dumb dogs; their watchmen were blind, given to excess, slothfulness, and sleep."[8] John Knox knew that continued reformation in the Church was impossible unless God was pleased to grant the gift of faithful pastors to His people.

While John Knox was dying, he was much engaged in meditation and prayer. One day he ordered his faithful servant, Richard Bannatyne, to order his coffin to be made. During that same day, he was much in prayer, his thoughts clearly on the future of the Church. "Be merciful, Lord to thy Church, which thou has redeemed. Give peace to this afflicted commonwealth. *Raise up faithful pastors* who will take the charge of thy Church."[9] A few days later, on the Lord's day, a number of people came to visit him after the sermon. Again, he was in prayer, "Lord, *grant true pastors* to thy Church, that purity of doctrine may be retained."[10]

Several centuries later, George Whitefield commented that churches are dead because dead men preach to them. John Knox knew nothing of this kind of spiritual lethargy, and he understood well that if it was tolerated in the churches at all, the results would be spiritually disastrous.

The gift of faithful pastors is a coronation gift to the Church from Christ Jesus, enthroned in heaven. "And He Himself gave some to be apostles, some prophets, some evangelists, and some pastors and teachers, for the equipping of the saints for the work of ministry, for the edifying of the body of Christ (Ephesians 4:11–12)." The book of Ephesians was dear to Knox, and he knew that the restoration of the Church was not going to be accomplished without pastors. By the grace of God, in the early years of the Reformation in Scotland, Protestant teaching had spread largely by means of smuggled literature. Luther and Tyndale had both had their influence. For many years, there were no public teachers of the Word there. But when the sentiments of the Reformation were generally adopted by many (through the instrumentality of literature), the first obvious need the new believers had was the need for pastors.

Some things never change. As we have noted earlier, our need of the hour is not necessarily men with identical gifts and abilities as Knox. But the need for godly and educated men, men who fear God and nothing else, is always a constant need. In a letter of "Wholesome Counsel" to the believers in Scotland before the Reformation had burst out of hiding, Knox counseled them to behave prudently in their gatherings, and in such as way as might reveal to them those who were gifted and called. When the Church is without faithful pastors, the prayer and lament and search should be for faithful pastors. "And then let some place of scripture be plainly and distinctly read, so much as shall be thought sufficient for the day or time; which ended, if any brother have exhortation, question, or doubt, let him not fear to speak and move the same, so that he do it with moderation, either to edify or be edified. And hereof I doubt not but that great profit shall shortly ensue . . . the judgments and spirits of men shall be tried, their patience and modesty shall be known; and, finally, *their gifts and utterance shall appear.* Multiplication of words, prolix interpretations, and willfulness in reasoning are to be avoided at all times."[11]

It would be hard to imagine a more pitiful situation—a small gathering of believers, a copy of the Bible, and no specified leadership. And yet Knox understood that Christ was the Giver of gifts to the Church, and this included pastors for His Church. Whenever God's people are gathered in His name, they have the authority of His Word to seek His blessing in their midst. The Lord Himself instructed us to pray in this fashion, toward this end. "Then He said to His disciples, 'The harvest truly is plentiful, but the laborers are few. Therefore pray the Lord of the harvest to send out laborers into His harvest (Matthew 9:37–38).'"

In our prosperity, we have forgotten that Christ is the Lord of the harvest, the Lord of the pastoral office. We have bureaucratized the process, and have robbed the ministry of its potency, turning it into a certified indoor job with no heavy lifting. No longer a true ministry, the pastorate is considered a profession, whose gateway is an accredited graduate school, just like all the other respectable professions. None of this is to say that participation in our system is wrong or sinful, but it certainly makes us think that something must be wrong *somewhere.* It reminds us of the story of an Anglican vicar who said that everywhere the apostle Paul went there was either a revival or a riot, but that everywhere *he* went, tea was served.

And so our prayer should be the same as that of the dying Knox, "Lord, grant faithful pastors, men who will preach and teach, in season and out of season. Lord, give us men who would gladly preach their next sermon even if it meant going to the stake for it. Lord, give us men who will hate all falsehood and lies, whether in the Church or out of it. Lord, grant to your struggling Church men who fear You above all."

Lord, give us men who will lead in accordance with Your Word.

THE LESSONS OF LEADERSHIP

1. A leader must know how to love.
2. A leader reveres the Lord of heaven.
3. Courage is the testing point of all the virtues, and a leader must have it.
4. Strength of character in leadership is tempered with mercy.
5. Strong leadership must always be balanced.
6. A leader must understand tenderness.
7. Men with gifts in leadership must also have the gift of humility.
8. Great leaders are often those who attract great enemies.
9. A leader must always be a student.
10. True humor is a great asset in leadership.
11. The one who would command obedience must himself be obedient.
12. A leader in the Church must be a churchman.
13. A leader is patient.
14. A leader understands the leadership exhibited in other eras, and understands the importance of tradition.
15. A leader will love his nation.
16. A leader in the theological arena must understand theology.
17. A leader works together with other leaders.

18. Leadership understands the importance of vision.
19. A leader pours himself into his work.
20. A leader knows how to be provocative.
21. Leadership must be clear-minded.
22. Leadership begins in the home.
23. A leader is a virtuous man.
24. A leader who loves what is right must know how to hate what is wrong.
25. A leader must know how to communicate what he understands.
26. Prophetic understanding is essential to leadership.
27. Leaders cannot be bought.
28. A leader must understand and admit his faults and failings.
29. A good leader knows how to die.
30. A leader is a man who fills the call of greatness without becoming filled with himself.

Notes

Introduction

1. Dorothy Parker, *The Poetry & Short Stories of Dorothy Parker* (New York: The Modern Library, 1994), 107.
2. C.S. Lewis, *English Literature in the Sixteenth Century* (Oxford: Clarendon Press, 1954), 198.

Part 1: The Life of John Knox

1. Thomas McCrie, *Life of John Knox* (Edinburgh and London: W. Blackwood & Sons, 1865), 9.
2. Henry Cowan, *John Knox: The Hero of the Scottish Reformation* (1905; reprint, New York: AMS Press, 1970), 15. A short sketch of Winzet's character can be found in C.S. Lewis, *English Literature in the Sixteenth Century*, 202–3.
3. Not to be confused with his nephew and successor.
4. Thomas McCrie, *Life of John Knox*, 14.
5. Not to be confused with Elizabeth II, who is reigning in England right now.
6. Kevin Reed, "John Knox: The Forgotten Reformer" (Dallas: Presbyterian Heritage Publications, forthcoming), 25.
7. This was the view that defended the decrees of the Council of Constance, and the liberties of the Gallican church, over against the papacy. One of the most common modern errors about the medieval period is the assumption that papal claims were unquestioned and unchallenged. But Major was no Protestant, and yet staunchly opposed the claims of the papacy. In this, he had much in common with many medieval thinkers.
8. Terry Johnson, ed., *Leading in Worship* (Oak Ridge, TN: The Covenant Foundation, 1996), 121. The emphasis is mine.

9. C.S. Lewis, *English Literature in the Sixteenth Century*, 32–3. I strongly recommend that anyone serious about the study of the Reformation era read the Introduction to this book. It is simply priceless.

10. P. Hume Brown, *John Knox: A Biography* (London: Adam and Charles Black, 1895), 65.

11. Henry Cowan, *John Knox*, 54–5.

12. John Knox, *History of the Reformation in Scotland*, vol. 1, ed. William Croft Dickinson (New York: Philosophical Library, 1950), 63–4.

13. Thomas McCrie, *Life of John Knox*, 21. This is as good a time as any to apologize for the variations of spelling and usage. Different sources modernize the language and spelling in different ways and to differing extent. "Bairnes" refers to Knox's pupils, and "ane" means one.

14. Thomas McCrie, *The Story of the Scottish Church* (1874; reprint, Glasgow: Free Presbyterian Publications, 1988), 20–1.

15. John Knox, *History of the Reformation in Scotland*, vol. 1, 76.

16. Ibid., 77–8.

17. Ibid., 79.

18. C.S. Lewis, *English Literature in the Sixteenth Century*, 201.

19. John Woodbridge, ed., *Great Leaders of the Christian Church* (Chicago: Moody Press, 1988), 252.

20. Ibid., 351.

21. C.S. Lewis, *English Literature in the Sixteenth Century*, 202.

22. Thomas McCrie, *Life of John Knox*, 22.

23. John Knox, *History of the Reformation in Scotland*, vol. 1, 80.

24. Ibid., 81.

25. Ibid., 83.

26. Thomas McCrie, *Life of John Knox*, 29.

27. John Knox, *Selected Writings of John Knox* (Dallas: Presbyterian Heritage Publications, 1995), 9.

28. John Knox, *History of the Reformation in Scotland*, vol. 1, 95.

29. John Rough had left the castle before it was besieged and made his way to England. He supported himself and his wife by knitting caps and stockings. He was elected the pastor of a church in hiding, which was betrayed to the authorities a few weeks later. He was tried and burned at the stake in December of 1557. He was a simple man, and a wonderful Christian.

30. W.H. Lewis in *Essays Presented to Charles Williams* (Grand Rapids, MI: Eerdmans, 1947), 136.

31. Ibid., 141–2. Quote uses "feet" instead of the American "foot" for length description.

32. Henry Cowan, *John Knox*, 83–4.

33. John Knox, *History of the Reformation in Scotland*, vol. 1, 97.

34. Ibid., 108.

35. Henry Cowan, *John Knox*, 85.

36. Thomas McCrie, *Life of John Knox*, 35.

37. Ibid., 109.

38. Henry Cowan, *John Knox*, 105.

39. This defense is available in John Knox, *Selected Writings of John Knox*, 19–64.

40. Thomas McCrie, *Life of John Knox*, 44.

41. Ibid., 55.

42. Ibid., 59.

43. Ibid., 61.

44. Even C.S. Lewis, who admires Knox with a little reluctance, raises this question of the nature of his courage, ". . . these fiery exhortations are uttered by man in safety to men in horrible danger." C.S. Lewis, *English Literature in the Sixteenth Century*, 198.

45. Thomas McCrie, *Life of John Knox*, 72.

46. Henry Cowan, *John Knox*, 131.

47. Thomas McCrie, *Life of John Knox*, 80.

48. Henry Cowan, *John Knox*, 164.

49. John Knox, *Selected Writings of John Knox*, 447.

50. Ibid., 448.

51. Thomas McCrie, *Life of John Knox*, 91.

52. Ibid., 92.

53. Ibid., 93.

54. C.S. Lewis in *Essays Presented to Charles Williams* (Grand Rapids, MI: Eerdmans, 1947), 138–9.

55. John Piper, *Future Grace* (Sisters, OR: Multnomah Publications, 1995), 171–2.

56. Henry Cowan, *John Knox*, 149.

57. Ibid., 151.

58. John Howie, *The Scots Worthies* (1870; reprint, Edinburgh: Banner of Truth, 1995), 52.

59. Thomas McCrie, *Life of John Knox*, 125.

60. Ibid., 125–6.
61. John Knox, *History of the Reformation in Scotland*, vol. 1, 181.
62. Thomas McCrie, *Life of John Knox*, 131.
63. Ibid., 146.
64. Ibid., 154.
65. Otto Scott, *James I: The Fool as King* (Vallecito, CA: Ross House Books, 1976), 17.
66. Henry Cowan, *John Knox*, 268.
67. Thomas McCrie, *Life of John Knox*, 182.
68. Henry Cowan, *John Knox*, 273.
69. Thomas McCrie, *Life of John Knox*, 187.
70. Ibid., 187.
71. Henry Cowan, *John Knox*, 279.
72. Ibid., 280.
73. Thomas McCrie, *Life of John Knox*, 207–8.
74. Henry Cowan, *John Knox*, 80.
75. Kevin Reed, ed., *The Scottish Confession of Faith (1560)* (Dallas: Presbyterian Heritage Publications, 1992), 6. This quote is taken from the publisher's introduction.
76. Ibid., 10–1.
77. Kevin Reed, ed., "The First and Second Books of Discipline" (Dallas: Presbyterian Heritage Publications, forthcoming), 70–1.
78. Thomas McCrie, *Life of John Knox*, 185.
79. Tony Curto, "John Knox: The Watchman of Scotland," Antithesis 1, no. 3, (1990): 17.
80. Otto Scott, *James I*, 18.
81. Ibid., 23.
82. Ibid., 34.
83. Ibid., 44.
84. Thomas McCrie, *Life of John Knox*, 239.
85. Ibid., 248.
86. Ibid.
87. Ibid., 264.
88. Ibid., 271.
89. Ibid., 276–7.
90. Otto Scott, *James I*, 72.
91. John Knox, *Selected Writings of John Knox*, inside cover.

PART 2: THE CHARACTER OF JOHN KNOX

1. John Knox, *Selected Writings of John Knox*, 73.
2. Ibid., 75.
3. Thomas McCrie, *Life of John Knox*, 75.
4. Ibid., 27.
5. C.S. Lewis, *English Literature in the Sixteenth Century*, 198.
6. Ambrose Bierce once defined the noun rear, in military matters, as "that exposed part of the army that is nearest to Congress." Ambrose Bierce, *The Devil's Dictionary* (New York: Dover Publications, 1958), 107.
7. Thomas McCrie, *Life of John Knox*, 61.
8. Diarmaid MacCulloch, *Thomas Cranmer: A Life* (New Haven, CT: Yale University Press, 1996), 603.
9. John Knox, *Selected Writings of John Knox*, 141.
10. Ibid., inside back flyleaf.
11. Thomas McCrie, *Life of John Knox*, 278.
12. Ibid., 288.
13. John Knox, *Selected Writings of John Knox*, 302.
14. Ibid., 450–1.
15. Thomas McCrie, *Life of John Knox*, 288.
16. David Hay Fleming, *Critical Reviews Relating Chiefly to Scotland* (London: Hodder and Stoughton, 1912), 203.
17. C.S. Lewis, *English Literature in the Sixteenth Century*, 39.
18. Loraine Boettner, *The Reformed Doctrine of Predestination* (Phillipsburg, NJ: Presbyterian and Reformed Publishing Co., 1963), 381.
19. John Knox, *Selected Writings of John Knox*, 73.
20. Some might want to argue that Knox was an extremist on predestination simply because he believed in it, but this approach has disadvantages, among them the labeling of many of the Church's greatest thinkers as extremists. Knox's position on this was theologically moderate, but fully biblical. He was unquestionably and fully "Calvinistic."
21. Thomas McCrie, *Life of John Knox*, 33.
22. Ibid., 74.
23. Ibid., 207.

24. Ibid., 37.

25. John Knox, *Selected Writings of John Knox*, 108–9.

26. Ibid., 121.

27. Ibid., 570.

28. C.S. Lewis, *English Literature in the Sixteenth Century*, 202.

29. To give Lewis credit for consistency, the demeanor he objects to in Knox, he also objects to it when he finds it in Scripture. See C.S. Lewis, *Reflections on the Psalms* (London: Collins, 1958), 23–33. In other words, Knox could defend himself from Scripture on this point, and Lewis would have granted that Knox was genuinely imitating what he saw in Scripture.

30. John Knox, *Selected Writings of John Knox*, 227.

31. Ibid.

32. C.S. Lewis, *English Literature in the Sixteenth Century*, 32–3.

33. John Knox, *Selected Writings of John Knox*, 61.

34. Ibid., 230.

35. Ibid., 228.

36. Ibid., 275.

37. Thomas McCrie, *Life of John Knox*, 279.

38. Ibid., 218.

39. C.S. Lewis, *English Literature in the Sixteenth Century*, 55.

40. Thomas McCrie, *Life of John Knox*, 11.

41. John Knox, *Selected Writings of John Knox*, 37.

42. Thomas McCrie, *Life of John Knox*, 69.

43. Henry Cowan, *John Knox*, 135–6.

44. Thomas McCrie, *Life of John Knox*, 106.

45. Ibid., 287.

46. Ibid., 271.

47. Jones and Wilson, *Angels in the Architecture* (Moscow, ID: Canon Press, 1998), 69–78.

48. C.S. Lewis, *English Literature in the Sixteenth Century*, 201.

49. John Knox, *History of the Reformation in Scotland*, vol. 1, 181.

50. Ibid., 128.

51. Ibid., 73.

52. Ibid.

53. Ibid.

54. John Knox, *Selected Writings of John Knox*, 465–6

55. Thomas McCrie, *Life of John Knox*, 96.

56. Ibid., 97.
57. Ibid., 104.
58. John Knox, *History of the Reformation in Scotland*, vol. 1, 155.
59. Thomas McCrie, *Life of John Knox*, 50.
60. Ibid., 49.
61. John Knox, *Selected Writings of John Knox*, 106–7.
62. Thomas McCrie, *Life of John Knox*, 51.
63. John Knox, *Selected Writings of John Knox*, 297–8.
64. Ibid., 299.
65. Ibid., 315.
66. Ibid., 344.
67. Ibid., 343.
68. Ibid., 88–9.
69. Ibid., 208–9.
70. Loraine Boettner, *The Reformed Doctrine of Predestination* , 379.
71. Ibid.
72. Thomas McCrie, *Life of John Knox*, 269.
73. John Knox, *Selected Writings of John Knox*, 186.
74. Ibid., 503.
75. Ibid., 492.
76. ". . . the most part of Germany, the country of Helvetia, the king of Denmark, the nobility of Poland, together with many other cities and churches reformed, appeal from the tyranny of that Antichrist, and most earnestly do call for a lawful and general council, wherein all controversies in religion may be decided by the authority of God's most sacred word." John Knox, *Selected Writings of John Knox*, 475.
77. Thomas McCrie, *Life of John Knox*, 7.
78. John Knox, *Selected Writings of John Knox*, 165–6.
79. Ibid., 206.
80. Ibid., 369.
81. Ibid., 505.
82. Ibid., 119.
83. Junius Brutus, *A Defence of Liberty Against Tyrants* (Edmonton, AB: Still Water Revival Books, 1989).
84. Thomas McCrie, *Life of John Knox*, 4.
85. Ibid., 52.
86. John Knox, *Selected Writings of John Knox*, 118.

87. Ibid., 148.
88. Martin Luther, *Bondage of the Will* (n.p.: Fleming H. Revell Co., 1957), 319.
89. It is interesting to note that Knox embarrasses some of his later biographers on this point. For example, see Henry Cowan, *John Knox*, 153–5.
90. Ibid., 152.
91. John Knox, *Selected Writings of John Knox*, 352.
92. Ibid., 527.
93. Ibid., 548.
94. Ibid., 256.
95. J.C. Ryle, *Five English Reformers* (Carlisle, PA: Banner of Truth, 1960), 91.
96. Ibid., 105.
97. Thomas McCrie, *Life of John Knox*, 53.
98. Ibid., 281–2.
99. Ibid., 284.
100. Ibid.
101. John Knox, *Selected Writings of John Knox*, 600.
102. Ibid., 182–3.
103. Kevin Reed, "John Knox: The Forgotten Reformer," 40.
104. John Knox, *Selected Writings of John Knox*, 236.
105. Ibid., 599.
106. Ibid., 243.
107. Ibid., 268.
108. Ibid., 238.
109. Ibid., 237.
110. Ibid., 253.
111. Thomas McCrie, *Life of John Knox*, 107.
112. C.S. Lewis, *English Literature in the Sixteenth Century*, 199.
113. Ibid., 200.
114. John Knox, *Selected Writings of John Knox*, 369.
115. Ibid., 456.
116. Thomas McCrie, *Life of John Knox*, 86.
117. Ibid., 184.
118. Ibid., 211.
119. Antonia Fraser, *Mary Queen of Scots* (New York: Delta Books, 1969), 433.
120. Henry Cowan, *John Knox*, 141.

121. Thomas McCrie, *Life of John Knox*, 56.
122. Ibid., 217.
123. John Knox, *Selected Writings of John Knox*, 185.
124. Ibid., 331.
125. Thomas McCrie, *Life of John Knox*, 296–7.
126. John Knox, *Selected Writings of John Knox*, 223.
127. Ibid., 561.
128. R. Tudur Jones, "Preacher of Revolution," Christian History 14, no. 2 (1995): 17.
129. Thomas McCrie, *Life of John Knox*, 287.
130. Ibid.
131. Loraine Boettner, *The Reformed Doctrine of Predestination*, 374.
132. Antonia Fraser, *Mary Queen of Scots*, 154.
133. R. Tudur Jones, "Preacher of Revolution," Christian History 14, no. 2 (1995): 8.
134. John Knox, *Selected Writings of John Knox*, 212–3.
135. Ibid., 63.
136. Ibid., 204–5.
137. Ibid., 213.
138. Thomas McCrie, *Life of John Knox*, 286.
139. Ibid., 92.
140. John Knox, *Selected Writings of John Knox*, 447.
141. Ibid., 351.
142. Kevin Reed, "John Knox: The Forgotten Reformer," 185.
143. Ibid., 193.
144. Ibid.
145. Ibid., 194.
146. Ibid.
147. Quintilian, *Institutio Oratoria*, vol. 1 (Cambridge, MA: Harvard University Press, 1920), 9.
148. John Knox, *History of the Reformation in Scotland*, vol. 1, 65.
149. John Knox, *Selected Writings of John Knox*, 205.
150. Thomas McCrie, *Life of John Knox*, 291–2.
151. Ibid., 35.
152. Ibid., 249.
153. Ibid., 294.
154. John Knox, *Selected Writings of John Knox*, 73.
155. Henry Cowan, *John Knox*, 377.
156. Thomas McCrie, *Life of John Knox*, 254.

157. Ibid., 272.
158. Antonia Fraser, *Mary Queen of Scots*, 98.
159. John Calvin, *Letters of John Calvin* (Carlisle, PA: Banner of Truth, 1980), 237.
160. Thomas McCrie, *Life of John Knox*, 287.
161. C.S. Lewis, *English Literature in the Sixteenth Century*, 202.
162. Thomas McCrie, *Life of John Knox*, 143.
163. Ibid., 272.
164. Ibid., 275.
165. Ibid., 97.
166. Ibid., 279–280.
167. Ibid., 286.
168. Ibid., 289.

Part 3: The Legacy of John Knox

1. John Knox, *History of the Reformation in Scotland*, vol. 1, vii.
2. Morton Smith, *Studies in Southern Presbyterian Theology* (Phillipsburg, NJ: Presbyterian and Reformed Publishing Co., 1962), 19.
3. Douglas Kelly, *The Emergence of Liberty in the Modern World* (Phillipsburg, NJ: Presbyterian and Reformed Publishing Co., 1992), 132.
4. Ibid., 52.
5. Ibid., 123.
6. David Hay Fleming, *Critical Reviews Relating Chiefly to Scotland*, 188–9.
7. John Knox, *Selected Writings of John Knox*, 587.
8. Ibid., 588.
9. Thomas McCrie, *Life of John Knox*, 274. The emphasis is mine.
10. Ibid., 275. The emphasis is still mine.
11. John Knox, *Selected Writings of John Knox*, 332.

Selected Bibliography

Brown, P. Hume. *John Knox: A Biography.* London: Adam and Charles Black, 1895.

Cowan, Henry. *John Knox: The Hero of the Scottish Reformation.* 1905; reprint, New York: AMS Press, 1970.

Fleming, David Hay. *Critical Reviews Relating Chiefly to Scotland.* London: Hodder and Stoughton, 1912.

———. *Mary Queen of Scots.* London: Hodder and Stoughton, 1897.

Fraser, Antonia. *Mary Queen of Scots.* New York: Bantam Doubleday Dell, 1969.

Knox, John. *History of the Reformation in Scotland,* vol. 1. Edited by William Croft Dickinson. New York: Philosophical Library, 1950.

———. *Selected Writings of John Knox.* Dallas: Presbyterian Heritage Publications, 1995.

Lewis, C.S. *English Literature in the Sixteenth Century.* Oxford: Clarendon Press, 1954.

MacCulloch, Diarmaid. *Thomas Cranmer: A Life.* New Haven, CT & London: Yale University Press, 1996.

McCrie, Thomas. *Life of John Knox.* Edinburgh and London: W. Blackwood & Sons, 1865.

———. *The Story of the Scottish Church.* 1874; reprint, Glasgow: Free Presbyterian Publications, 1988.

Reed, Kevin. "John Knox: The Forgotten Reformer." Dallas: Presbyterian Heritage Publications, forthcoming.

Woodbridge, John ed. *Great Leaders of the Christian Church.* Chicago: Moody Press, 1988.